THE HEALING SANDWICH

DR. HOPE TELEPOVA

Editing, design, distribution by Bublish
Published by Dr. Hope Nadezhda Telepova
ISBN: 979-8-89989-112-0 (paperback)
ISBN: 979-8-89989-111-3 (eBook)

TABLE OF CONTENTS

THE WORD FROM THE EDITOR

I have known Nadezhda Nikolayevna (it is the way we address our teachers in Russia – by their first and middle names) for a long time. She was my English teacher for four years in Russia, and we stayed in touch after I graduated. For more than twenty years we did not see each other until our paths crossed in the summer of 2025 when I spent a few days in Miami, where she currently lives. We met for lunch and had a wonderful time reminiscing and catching up. At the end of our meal, Nadezhda asked if I would help her with the English version of her book. Naturally, I agreed—how could I refuse the chance to support my favorite English teacher, especially since I have been living in North America and speaking English for so long?

Working on this book turned out to be a deeply therapeutic experience. As I read, I understood why Nadezhda felt compelled to make her work available in English. Though we may live in different places, speak different languages, and belong to diverse cultures, the challenges of family life and relationships with people unite us. These issues are universal and experienced in strikingly similar ways across the world. For centuries, the conflict between fathers and sons has remained unresolved, and Nadezhda's book resonates with that timeless struggle.

When she first moved to the United States, Nadezhda did not immediately consider translating her book into English. But living here and connecting with people helped her realize that, although Americans may speak a different language, they face the same relationship patterns. Her Healing Sandwich Method offers a way to mend wounds, strengthen bonds, and enrich lives.

The healing power of her work is felt through every word and paragraph, as you relive the stories and apply the techniques to your own experiences. For me, reading this book was transformative. I hope it brings you the same sense of insight and renewal. Enjoy.

Yulia Siminic

INTRODUCTION

Let's stop blaming our parents. It is not their fault. The truth is that you do not need years of therapy on unpacking most of your childhood traumas to live happily, to achieve success, and to experience fulfillment. There is another way. I am here to share techniques that can give you the support you need on this important journey.

You might be surprised. After all, the dominant narrative in the pop psychology today tells us the exact opposite:

- ☹ "Struggling with fulfillment in life? - It is your parents' fault, because they traumatized you when you were growing up and programmed you for failure!"

- ☹ "Unable to develop healthy relationships? - It must be an unresolved rejection trauma from your childhood!"

- ☹ "Experiencing difficulties to separate from your parents to live your own life? You are doomed."

- ☹ "Are you always busy helping your parents and putting their needs ahead of yours? - That is an emotional role-reversal."

☹ "Deep attachment to your parents can sometimes overshadow the needs of your own children—leaving them feeling unseen or emotionally underserved."

☹ "You do not like talking to your parents because they disciplined you too much? - You can stop communicating with them."

That is just a glimpse of what is flooding the media space nowadays around parent-child relationships. Once someone buys into this mindset, they often get hooked on never-ending "working on themselves and digging their wounds."

Not too long ago, I came across a reel by a young woman joking about her experience with one of the specialists. She said:

> *"I'm kinda over therapy, at least in the way it's pushed now. It feels more like a club for the emotionally addicted. Psychology was supposed to help people live better, not to escape life through doing therapy as it is happening today. Nowadays it feels more like a cult: 'bring a friend and we'll heal together.' Not my cup of tea. I'm out."*

To be frank, she has a point.

Too often, some specialists get people hooked on long-term processing of unresolved trauma, unpacking emotional wounds, and endless "inner" work on yourself. If that sounds familiar, it is time to call it a day.

In my opinion, sometimes it is a great business model which peddles pseudo-truths about your 'inner wounds' to foster emotional dependency and keep you financially tethered to a cycle that profits from your "unresolved childhood trauma".

I'm not speaking as an outsider.

I've spent almost four decades in education and psychology; over thirty years of researching, working on my Ph.D., giving lectures, conducting workshops, and counseling in a wide range of countries. Most of my experience and knowledge was gained through my professional work in Russia. Nevertheless, speaking at seminars and conferences in other countries — including Ukraine, Kazakhstan, Armenia, Lithuania, Switzerland, Spain, China, Turkey, Germany, Canada, the United States, and others -I realized that resentment is a universal trap, holding people back from emotional well-being regardless of culture or geography. Resentment often deepens through modern practices in which people endlessly unpack and process their wounds. And everywhere I go, I see the damage done by keeping the phase of exploring past trauma alive longer than necessary

There's even a meme going around:

> *"I went to a long-term therapy, as a result I lost all my friends and family, but hey, at least, now I have boundaries and my truth"*

That is what happens when an individual seeks help for personal, family, or professional matters and instead is pulled into endless revisiting and unpacking unresolved trauma by:

- processing the early attachment to the mother and unresolved maternal issues.

- working through paternal complex and father wounds.

- healing the 'inner child'.

- cutting ties with 'toxic' people including family members.

Though it begins with a sense of empowerment, it often unravels into emotional spiraling, isolation, and lingering bitterness and pain. Deep pain.

On the other side of this process there are heartbroken and rejected parents. They are faced with numerous accusations from their child and left lost and confused.

There are two extremes:

The first one: *"If you want to keep the relationship, don't bring up any issues."*

BUT: unresolved issues don't just go away; they fester; avoiding honest conversations is the beginning of emotional disconnection and mental distress for the one who stays silent.

Another extreme: *"Be straightforward and say how you feel without any sugarcoating. Be blunt and don't worry if what you say hurts anyone."* It also leads to disconnection.

You might hear someone preaching *"Speak the truth in love"*- wisdom. It can *sound so* good. But what does it really mean?

Should you develop *skills verbally hurting people in a soft, sweet voice?* Will it help? Of course not.

So, what should we do?

Over the past thirty years of practice, I developed a method of my own. I call it **"Sandwich, Healing Resentment"** or just **"The Healing Sandwich"**

That is what this book is all about.

Using this technique will help you find the *middle ground,* the place where you are not bottling your pain, not suppressing the truth, and not damaging your relationships either.

You will not hurt yourself or others.

Is this a magic wand that instantly fixes everything? - No.

It is a mechanism and once you learn it, I can assure you: you'll find peace of mind and emotional clarity.

Why a *sandwich*?

Nourishment is essential for our everyday lives. **Gratitude, forgiveness, and blessing** are the key ingredients of the Healing Sandwich and they are essential for our social, personal, spiritual and physical life.

This technique wasn't created overnight. My husband and I developed it together over 30 years of working with:

- Married couples,

- People struggling with addictions and codependency,

- Teens and their parents,

- Adult children and their aging parents.

This approach is universal. It helps rebuild relationships in nearly every context: between parents and children, spouses, coworkers, managers and employees, friends, and even casual acquaintances if there is a desire to have a good relationship with one another. It's a life raft for your emotional state, something you can rely on, no matter what is happening around you.

Throughout this book, you will walk with me into the world of **classic psychology,** the one that existed before today's loud "unpacking trauma" voices.

You'll step into the life stories of real people, and you'll witness transformation, not through magic, but through the power of *the Healing Sandwich*. And I believe, deep down, something in these stories will resonate with you. Because we're all humans, with shared values, and similar messiness. With these stories, you'll learn how to apply this method **if** you're willing to try.

Out of respect for privacy, all names and personal details have been changed. Still, hundreds, maybe thousands of you will recognize yourselves on these pages. That's not a coincidence. It's the truth of when toxic emotions make lives look painfully alike.

How do we change that?

You will learn how **to turn your crap into a fertilizer**. (That's what my husband used to call it, transforming life's mess into something that makes beauty growth possible.)

Who should read this book?

- It's for adult children who sense something off about all the current conversation about detachment from their parents and endless inner work, and who are looking for a solid foundation to push back against all this noise. I hope you will find the answers in this book and follow the way out of your life's labyrinth.

- It's for estranged moms and dads who have been left behind, cut off by their grown children following the popular trend. This book will help you understand what's happening and guide you through the grief of having "prodigal children."

- It's for anyone drowning in anger and resentment.

Make no mistake, clinging to resentment; it traps you in your own suffering. And when you become stuck in that emotional swamp, every part of life starts falling apart even if it doesn't seem that way at first.

Throughout this book, you'll find true stories that will illustrate how to avoid that trap and yes, **how to turn your life's crap into fertilizer**.

Wishing you wisdom and love, dear reader.

Chapter One

ABOUT "MOTHER FIGURE", "INNER CHILD" AND SIMILAR METHODS

"My hatred fills me up entirely! I can't take this anymore!"

Her fists clenched, lips trembling. A young lady looked like a coiled spring about to snap. I was sitting in a chair in front of the room, where I finished giving a seminar. There were people all around us. Some folks were there to ask questions; others came to share their personal experiences and thank me; some sought clarification on a few points raised during my presentation. I saw a woman close to me- waiting patiently for her turn to speak. But then this young lady had stormed into the circle uninvited, towering over me.

"And I hate you too!" She blurted out.

I did not respond to her looking straight in her eyes. There, I saw turmoil—a battle between rage and despair; pain buried deep inside. She didn't seem to care that so many strangers became witnesses to her outburst.

"You're always talking about choice!" She nearly shouted. "So, according to you, I chose this hell I'm living in? Seriously? I wake up hating the world, and I am overwhelmed by all the hatred I feel. I no longer can fall asleep at night because my insides are twisting with pain. And this is all my own choice?!"

Silence enveloped the room. I noticed the seminar organizer taking a step toward her, ready to ask the poor girl to go outside and calm down. I shook my head slightly as a sign to leave her alone.

"Who else do you hate so much, besides me?" I asked.

"My mother! The woman who dares to call herself my mother! She ruined my life when I was fourteen. She told me that my dad was not my biological father. Apparently, she had a fling with a guy on her vacation when she was young and got pregnant. Nothing has been the same for me since I heard this news! It's been four years now, and no one—NO ONE—can help me! Not even my therapist! My trauma is too deep, and I am having difficulties to unpack it!"

(Oh, how much pain she was carrying…)

Her voice cracked and trembled, but she caught herself. Using the techniques of physiological self-regulation- inhaling deeply and exhaling slowly—she unclenched her fists, shook off her hands to release tension, and continued to speak with her voice lower now:

"It's all her fault! I can't even love anyone. I had a wonderful man propose to me, and I want to marry him, but how can I love him! I can't imagine being a wife or a mother! I am so bitter! I feel so much pain and it is all because of my mother!"

(...she sounded like a broken record...)

"What exactly happened four years ago? What made your mother reveal this secret?" I asked.

"My dad left her for another woman! He left—my dad; I could not believe it! He is my dad to me. I always felt like his own daughter. Nearly twenty years ago, he forgave my mother because he loved her, and he never let the secret slip. Why did she have to tell me? I was already hurting so much from losing my father to a nurse at his hospital, who seduced him. I struggled to cope with this new blow. As he walked away, he didn't even look at my older brother and I..."

She got quiet, visibly fighting back tears. After a minute, her voice was cold when she said:

"And that evening, while we were having tea together, my mother brought more pain by revealing her secret. Who does that?"

She buried her face in her hands for a few seconds, then straightened up, fists clenched again. Looking down at me, she demanded:

"So, you are still going to tell me I chose to hate her? Or will you finally admit that HER actions made me hate her?"

"I can tell you why your mother did what she did."

Her eyes opened wide with both surprise and suspicion.

"I'll tell you why, do you want to know?" I asked again.

(God, help me now to wake her up, to lance this abscess.)

Without waiting for her reply, I paused, aligning my voice and tone with her pain and despair.

"Your mother saw how much you were hurting—her daughter, her dear child. She saw every cell of your soul ripped apart by the betrayal of the man you loved as a father. And so, she decided to make it worse by hurting you even more. She struck you with pain and then struck again saying: 'Here, take it, sweetie! More pain!'"

The girl recoiled in horror:

"Are you insane?! No! That's not true!"

"Of course not," I replied calmly.

She shook her head, pressing her fingers to her temples.

(Did I manage to awaken her mind?)

I asked:

"So why do you think your mother had that difficult conversation with you?"

"I don't know."

"Think again. How old were you then?"

"Fourteen."

"And your mother?"

"Thirty-six... no, thirty-seven."

"A young woman, left by her husband. A man who once forgave her mistake, but now abandoned her, shattering their family and betraying her and the kids. Could she be sure the secret from fifteen years ago would not resurface in a twisted version?"

"No..."

"So why did she do it?"

"To protect me...?"

(Half statement, half question. She's starting to think. Yes— Come on, break free from the web of lies, clear your mind!

"Your mom wanted to protect you—from what?"

"From lies."

"Because...?"

The girl stayed quiet, looking straight into my eyes.

"Because... she loves me very much."

Silence.

"And because she wanted me... to hear it from her."

A pause.

"And because she hoped I would understand her. And I...."

The girl choked back a sob. Nobody spoke a word and was watching intently.

"What's your name?" I asked.

"Dasha... My mom... I snap at her..."

Dasha pulled a tissue from her bag, blew her nose, and looked me in the eyes.

(There was a good curious gaze. A shadow of irritation flickered in her eyes.)

"But why didn't anyone tell me this over the past four years? Why did I spend all that time unpacking the pain from this trauma? Why was I forced to do that?!"

(My poor girl, you are yet another victim of the destructive "trauma digging").

"You heard me today speaking against the modern absurdity"

"Of course I did! That's what triggered me. And now I see I have been pulled along like an idiot all these years!"

(Dasha is winding up again.)

"Don't shift your hatred to a new target. Changing the players doesn't change the game. Remember that rule?"

She nodded.

"And remember, —switching cabins on the Titanic won't save you. You only survive by getting in a lifeboat. So, stop running from cabin to cabin on this sinking ship called "anger and resentment". The good news is, —you're done playing the victim in this game."

"So, what do I do now?" Tears welled up in Dasha's eyes again. "Where do I go from here? I hurt my mom so much…"

"Please, do not turn yourself into the next object of your hatred. Oh, do you really enjoy this game, huh?"

"No! I don't!"

(The girl woke up!)

"Then stop looking for the new targets to attack."

"Okay, I won't." She said with a smile.

(What a beautiful, radiant smile she has.)

Dasha was about to leave but suddenly spun back and hugged me tightly.

"Can I hug you? You have no idea what I'm feeling right now!"

(Oh, I do, my dear. I know how sweet it is when forgiveness and gratitude finally take root.)

As if reading my mind, Dasha asked:

"Do you think it's not too late to start making the Healing Sandwiches?"

"It's never too late…"

…At 4 a.m., my train was leaving that town. Dasha and her mother came to see me off.

"Thank you," said Dasha's mom.

"I love you," said Dasha.

We simply hugged goodbye.

I deeply love what I do.

Psychology—the science of the soul (*psyche* in Greek means "soul")—is an incredibly delicate field. Its purity depends entirely on the character and the integrity of the person who practices and communicates its truths.

Unfortunately, nowadays there's a growing trend of people entering this field without a solid academic foundation and/or without the intention of helping. Instead, some rely on quick-fix courses which are organized with the only purpose: to help newly made specialists earn money. From time to time, it can go sideways.

This approach creates a kind of "sectarian" mindset in psychology, where someone's entire understanding of this science is shaped by a single course (or a handful of them) and filtered through the biases of a specific instructor.

Just think about if we only tried to understand Language sciences solely through the rules of Punctuation (syntax);

or reduced Medicine to Proctology alone;

or viewed Philosophy exclusively through early Aristotle;

or learned Physics only through Einstein's theory of relativity…

This "course approach" has little in common with classical/academical science of psychology. Why is such an approach so popular? – because teaching someone to use a particular technique is far easier than giving them a solid foundation in multiple approaches, schools, and traditions of psychology which teaches them to think critically, to integrate and analyze what they learn. Building true expertise takes time. You cannot train a surgeon in a few weeks or months. And you certainly can't train a solid psychologist that quickly either. The soul is a far more delicate mechanism than a bone or a kidney. (As I've already mentioned, *"Psyche" means 'soul' in Greek; a psychologist is someone who works with the soul.*)

For those with a solid academic background, they would benefit from short-term courses that are excellent for professional development. But without that solid background, they run the risk of becoming a mass-production of "technicians"—like butchers or plumbers.

(Though to be fair, skilled plumbers are worth their weight in gold—*if* they're a real pro, not just someone fresh out of a weekend training.)

These "course-made specialists" often parrot the same slogans in different voices—male and female, baritone and soprano, young and old—until even the most absurd ideas start sounding like absolute truth:

- "Children didn't ask their parents to have them."

- "Only "kind love" should be used to raise kids. Discipline is dangerous."

- "You should always go in the direction your child chooses."

- "Energy flows from top to bottom. Parents should care for children all their life—but not the other way around."

- "If you turn toward your parents, you turn your back on your kids."

- "If you want to stay young, you should surround yourself only with young people. Stay away from your old, mature crowd."

- "Don't waste your life on people who criticize you. Stay close only to those who praise you."

- "If you outgrew your husband, it's time to divorce before he drags you down."

- "Your life depends on healing 'your inner child.'"

All these kinds of catchphrases, pushed through many media marketing scripts, are tearing families apart and destroying human relationships. They have nothing in common with classical fundamental psychology.

Besides they go directly against timeless values and divine laws of Love, which are laid out clearly in Scripture:

- *"What God has joined together, let no one separate"*—the value of marriage, loyalty, and faithfulness.

- *"Carry each other's burdens"*—the value of mutual support, learning, and accountability.

- *"Honor your father and mother"*—the value of family ties and generational continuity.

- *"Forgive, and you will be forgiven"*—liberation from bitterness and toxic emotions that poison relationships.

The "protocol practice" profits by manipulating toxic emotions; it is easy to make money on people who are dwelling in guilt, shame, fear, and resentment. Specialists earning money with such a protocol play on the basics:

- *"You're a terrible mother."*

- *"It's your fault your adult children are not successful in their lives"*

- *"You should take responsibility for your child's failing relationships and/or unsuccessful life."*

- *"By disciplining your child, you are creating a future abuser."*

- *"You should be fearful having children at all because you are a disaster."*

- *"It is your parents' fault when things go wrong in your life. They are responsible for your failures and your unhealthy relationships…"*

Once someone gets hooked, they begin to depend on constantly processing their search for whom-to- blame. And that can last for *years* in the interests of the trauma-digging specialists.

Long-term therapy isn't always needed—only when someone has a serious mental health condition diagnosed by a medical professional.

In this book, I'll give you a brief but meaningful overview of psychology and show how much of today's trend is far from the true science of psychology.

Psychology is incredibly multifaceted

Let's start with the simplest classification, three core approaches to psychological care:

Dynamic

Cognitive-Behavioral

Existential-Humanistic

We will examine four practical questions within each of them to illustrate how methods depend on the chosen approach of the specialist.

Question 1: What does the specialist focus on first when someone seeks help?

Question 2: What does the specialist see as the root cause of mental distress?

Question 3: What goal does the specialist set for their work with the client?

Question 4: What is the main strategy of the specialist in approaching the goal?

The Dynamic approach specialists focus on the unconscious (for instance, hidden memories influencing the present); see conflicts within the unconscious as the root cause of mental distress; their goal is to uncover and resolve the hidden meaning of inner conflicts; during sessions with the client they never give advice or recommendations, never evaluate anything, they maintain impartiality, work indirectly through free associations, dream analysis and/or fantasy analysis.

The Cognitive-Behavioral Approach specialists focus on the person's behavior, motivations, and awareness of their actions; consider destructive behaviors and faulty motivations as the reason for mental problems and distress; set the goal for correcting behavioral responses and activating constructive thinking and motivation. They act as advisors, problem-solvers, and offer evaluations ("good/bad, right/wrong").

The Existential-Humanistic Approach specialists focus on individual's personality, values, and search for meaning of life. They view alienation from self, others, and God as the cause of psycho and spiritual distress; they unlock personal potential. The goal of working with clients for these specialists is to help clients find their meaning in life, build a relationship of mutual acceptance, and authentic engagement.

How does the overview of classical psychology's main approaches assist you as a person who is not a psychologist?

When you seek help from different professionals, with the knowledge of the basics you won't be surprised to see different methods even when dealing with the same issue. You will stay grounded in the theoretical knowledge based on classical schools of thought, and throughout this book, I will refer back to them.

"Mother Figure" Technique

Let me warn you right away: my tone here will be openly skeptical. I want there to be no doubt about my opinion of such methods. So, if you're a fan of these techniques, you might want to stop reading and avoid disappointment. ☺ ☹

Let's start with the basic assumptions behind this technique:

☹ "Deep inside yourself lives a little 'inner child' who can be suffering because they did not receive enough love as a child".

☹ "You, a grown man or woman, can't fully live a fulfilling adult life because your 'inner tragic child' is still sobbing deep in your soul".

☹ "That 'inner child' was once abandoned by a 'not-quite-mother' and/or 'not-quite-father,' and was left to drown in the sea of emotional neglect".

☹ "Thus you still carry the image of these 'toxic parents' inside you, your life today is marked by failure and disappointment".

☹ "All countless 'traumatizing' events in your childhood created a 'bad mother figure' inside of you.

☹ "This 'figure' is living in you and it is destroying you and your life".

We do not speak now on PTSD (posttraumatic stress disorder) as there will be a special talk on it in chapter 5. But now let's look at some of the 'unbearably traumatic' childhood memories, often used in the 'mother figure' sessions (truth be told, everyone has these kinds of stories, but not everyone chooses to live in them):

"My mom and dad went to the movies and didn't take me! I wanted to go with them so badly! They left me with grandma! Sure, we played with her hide-and-seek and baked cookies, but still, I was so upset with my parent. It was a traumatic experience for me because I remember me sobbing uncontrollably for some time when they left!"

"I didn't want to go to daycare! I screamed and cried, but they left me there anyway for a whole day! Yeah, I had friends there and enjoyed being there with them, but I still remember how I cried when my mom dropped me off there! (Even though she kissed me goodbye!)"

"One time, I wanted to play with another child's toy car. But that boy wouldn't share. I begged, but mom said, 'It's not yours, you can't always have what you want.' So, I grabbed that toy anyway, and that child started crying. Mom yanked me away, and told dad about what happened, and I didn't get any sweets that night, but my brother did! I think that situation really impacted me. Ever since then, I can never go after what I want. I have a block."

...

So, one fine day some adult with such an 'unbearably traumatic' childhood hears that there is a miraculous specialist who 'heals inner children', it sounds promising for them, they go and voilà: get a blank check to dig endlessly through their 'deeply wounded' past. They hear what they like to hear: "you did not get the parents you deserved", "the only way to save the inner child (and yourself) is to build a new and more loving parent in your mind"

Then they start doing different exercises.

(I will give you an illustration of some of them).

Exercise 1: Restoring Your "Mother Figure"

You're asked to reflect on these incomplete statements:

- *"My childhood would have been much happier if my mom had…"*

- *"The most significant thing I lacked from my mother in childhood was …"*

- *"The most painful moment for me was when my mom…"*

Through these reflections, you're encouraged to steep yourself in dissatisfaction with your mother. The specialist gently insists:

"See? Now you're gaining insight into your true relationship with your mother. That's how it really was! Your inner child doesn't lie!"

"And this is just the beginning! You've never done long-term therapy before (oh, how could you?! But better late than never 😣). Imagine how deep your wounds are!"

"This work is important! Relationships with your mother are always complicated/relevant/life-defining/formative for all your other relationships. Without working on this issue, you will be stuck."

"I'll help you build an internal 'good mother.'"

The implicit message is:

☹ *Your mother is the root of all your misery.*

☹ *I, as a specialist, is the one to open your eyes and lead you to fulfillment and bliss.*

☹ *I am more reliable and loving than your real parents.*

☹ *Don't waste your time building a relationship with your actual mom, it's of no use and impossible! Instead, with my help, let's foster a bond between you and your inner child through a fantasy 'resource mother' we create together.*

Exercise 2: Creating Support for Your Inner Child

You are asked to 'support your inner child' by writing a letter from the perspective of your 'ideal mother'. You start to believe the following: "the reality is my own mother failed me, and the specialist keeps reinforcing my disappointment in her while encouraging me to imagine a created version of the mother I never had".

Your 'imaginary mother' writes (with your own hand) something like:

"My sweet girl... (or "boy", but let's be honest, it's mostly women who fall for this stuff)

"I know how much pain and loneliness you felt when I... (insert a situation where your real mother fell short of ' ideal').

"I am so sorry I was not there for you when you needed my kindness and support. I wasn't there for you. It pains me that I hurt you. You must have felt... (list as many anguished emotions as possible for maximum effect).

"Now, you can always count on me. I've changed. I've become more... (loving, caring, attentive—fill in all the traits of your imaginary perfect mom).

"I wish for you... (insert every desire, no matter how grand, since it's your 'ideal mom' talking to you), and I'll always be there to support you with your goals.

"I love you. I'm here for you. Forever yours, Mom (Not the real one, obviously)"

The underlying message:

☹ *"Your mom will never say this to you, so why even try to have that relationship?"*

☹ *"Just live in your mind, it's safer there".*

☹ *"Your mother is to blame for how you feel. Keep coming back to me (your specialist), because I'm the only one who understands you."*

You don't need a Ph.D. to see where this strategy leads.

At first sight, the 'mother figure' approach sounds like it is based on real events. But the truth is not so simple. People usually turn to specialists when they are already struggling with themselves, their relationships, their worldview, their understanding of God. In that condition, the brain is more likely to focus on the negative. The more depressed you are, the more critical you become, especially about your past. That is just how it works.

The method of processing the "mother/father figure" may look appealing. It can offer the chance to "transform" painful memories. But what is the real outcome? You double down on negativity toward your real mother. You start blaming her for everything wrong in your adult life. You feel stuck:

> *"It's all her fault. She will not change. I guess I'll never be happy."*

And that leads to the next trap, the craving for a "real" guru, a specialist with a magical cure switch to turn off the pain. But no such switch exists. And what about the little emotional highs from these exercises? It can resemble a sugar rush in your brain. It keeps you coming back for more, hooked on the "relief that only your specialist can offer".

In the hands of some gurus healing inner children your doubled negativity turns into imagined acts of aggression toward real parents. I heard people describe such exercises under their gurus supervision:

> *"Imagine your alcoholic father standing before you. Now you, as a child, grow larger towering over him as a giant. You can*

step on the alcoholic and he is gone! Free yourself from his power! You are stronger now. Do it! You're free!"

Or:

"Here's your mother the one who brought so much pain into your life. Watch her shrink into a tiny paper doll. She's nothing now. Get rid off her."

I've heard these and similar stories many times from people who came seeking help, plagued by panic attacks, fears, and depression. Their path into neurosis began during years with childhood trauma monetizers.

These practitioners often claim to work within the psychodynamic tradition. But let me assure you: they totally neglect and/or distort core principles of classical schools founded by Sigmund Freud, Alfred Adler, Erich Fromm, Carl Jung, Leopold Szondi, and others.

Classical psychoanalysis vs. Modern "Mother Figure" Trends

Sigmund Freud, the founder of classical psychoanalysis, believed that psychological discomfort of any kind arises from internal conflict between three "entities": the *Id*, the *Superego*, and the *Ego*.

- The **Id** represents instincts driving us toward pleasure, suppressing uncomfortable memories and rationalizing obvious personal failures (for instance, blaming one's inability to cook on "Mom never liked cooking / Mom liked cooking and forced me to cook," or blaming poor grades in physics on father "Dad was a blue color worker" or "Dad was a professor and had very high expectations of me").

- The **Superego** is a moral authority, a collection of rules and values inherited from parents and society that defines acceptable thoughts and behaviors (e.g., "you cannot have sex with every woman you desire" or "you must respect your parents and care for them").

- The **Ego** is our conscious self, managing behavior and trying to mediate between the demands of the *Id* and the restrictions of the *Superego* while maintaining harmony.

Freud argued that all psychological phenomena—emotions, reactions, behaviors—are shaped by prior experiences, childhood complexes, and traumas. But he also emphasized that uncovering these traumas isn't enough. The key lies in helping the person interpret them properly with the purpose of strengthening their *Ego*. When a trauma is discovered, the goal of psychological help is not to endlessly unpack it, but rather verbalize it, re-evaluate its significance, and recreate a new framework of beliefs. As a result, the painful memory often loses its relevance and may even fade entirely.

This is the exact opposite of what some "childhood trauma specialists' do today. Instead of helping clients move forward, they trap them in an endless loop of unpacking more and more wounds, blaming others, reliving past pain, and inventing "fantasy parents" or "a perfect childhood" to escape the reality of their actual life. That doesn't heal people; it makes them more reliant on their "guru" and more stuck in their pain and emotional struggles.

Adler's Perspective

Alfred Adler, founder of analytic individual psychotherapy, agreed with Freud on the importance of early childhood in shaping the unconscious. He described each person as having a "prototype", a primary way of adapting to life, formed before age five and later enriched with meanings and expectations that drive behavior.

Adler believed it's not the childhood events themselves, but one's **perceptions and expectations** of today that impact behavior the most. The wrong ones lead to feeling of inferiority, which is the main obstacle to personal growth. He called this set of flawed beliefs and thought patterns the "private logic."

For Adler, the goal of psychological help is to correct these distortions of meaning. A healthy psyche requires the development of a **social interest:** an active, positive engagement with the world around us. Adler defines three aspects of this interest:

- Belonging to home, family, and community (*social feeling*).

- Participating in the lives of others with respect and helpfulness (*socially oriented behavior*).

- Balancing personal needs and desires with those of others (*cognitive, socially oriented assumptions*: "Do unto others as you would have them do unto you").

What about modern "trauma healers" and "mother figure" enthusiasts? - Their methods are worlds apart from Adler's classic school.

Fromm's Humanistic Psychoanalysis

Erich Fromm distinguished between **productive** and **non-productive** orientations in life. A person's chosen orientation shapes their social character.

For instance:

- A **receptive orientation** (focused on taking from life) tends to breed a masochistic character type, driven by envy.

- An **exploitative orientation** (focused on dominating others) breeds a sadistic character type, driven by authoritarianism.

The psychologist's role, Fromm believed, is to guide clients toward a **productive orientation** and an abundant life. A productive orientation is one fueled by love and realized in striving toward its highest form of **agape** (unconditional love). Only this orientation allows an individual to satisfy their essential existential needs: closeness, rootedness, a system of values, and harmony with self.

So, the popular advice to sever ties, set harsh boundaries, and exile "toxic" family members runs directly counter to Fromm's philosophy.

Jung's Analytical Psychology

Carl Gustav Jung explored the deep forces of the unconscious, identifying several layers: personal, national, collective.

He saw **spiritual values** as the foundation of any psychotherapy, calling them universal and deeply rooted in the archetypical layers of the soul. Jung believed that values and meaning are unshakable, even though there are countless archetypes (patterns governing behavior).

For Jung, healing involves spontaneity and agape love that forgives and accepts. Jung emphasizes **building up**, not tearing down; **closeness**, not rigid boundaries.

Szondi's Fate Analysis

Leopold Szondi introduced the concept of the **familial unconscious:** a storehouse of ancestral values and aspirations. For Szondi, "fate" is a mix of inherited and freely chosen possibilities in life.

He identified five key domains of fate:

- choice concerning friends,

- choice concerning illness,

- choice concerning death style,

- choice concerning profession,

- choice concerning love and marriage.

In each, there's a **familial fate** (inherited patterns) and an **individual fate** (free choice).

Neither "inherited" means "bad" nor "free" means "good" and vice versa. For example, you can choose familial fate and follow healthy ancestral values (e.g., family loyalty, sobriety, care, forgiveness), in this case your life will go on with these values; but if you choose "individual fate", reject these values, go through lots of failures, start clinging to 'childhood traumas', nursing grievances against 'toxic righteous parents,' in this case you may find your life veering into bitterness and alienation. Your "free choice" may feel liberated, but it's ultimately self-defeating,

Conversely, you can break cycles of dysfunction in your familial fate (e.g. divorce, addiction, violence) with your individual fate by choosing to embrace values of commitment, forgiveness, and meaning.

A Personal Story of Choice

When my husband and I married over 40 years ago, both of our parents were divorced. For three generations on both sides, single motherhood was a repeating pattern.

At our wedding celebration, my husband suddenly stood up and said:

"Nadia, I know how painful it is to grow up without a father. I know how ugly divorce can be. I promise you. I will never say the vile word 'divorce'..." He paused and added: *"...at least not first."*

Overwhelmed by his passion, I also got up and said:

"I promise. I'll never say it first either."

He continued:

"And I vow that no matter what happens, I'll always share the same bed with you."

In first ten years of our life together, we faced three challenges where our marriage teetered on the brink of collapse. But each time, those vows held us together. I would provoke him: *"Go on! Say the word first!"* And he, standing firm, replied: *"I'm true to my promise. You won't hear the word from me. If you want to destroy this family, the ball is in your court. But count me out."*

Each time we made it through, our love deepened. My husband often joked: *"We managed to turn our life crap into fertilizer."*

We didn't realize it then, but on our wedding day we vowed **dedication: a** commitment to each other no matter what. Sticking to that choice wasn't about "compatibility" or "good character traits." It was about choice and living by that choice. We made our own "fate".

We had a great blessing on the tenth-year anniversary, when we attended a marriage conference; the speakers were spouses, an experienced couple who taught seminars on love, forgiveness, blessing, and dedication. That's when my husband and I caught the desire to do the same: to give families hope. Our logic was simple: if we managed to pass the tests of our dedication, any other family could do it too.

The secret is simple: make the right choice and live by it.

> EITHER you choose dedication to your marriage, and then you have a chance for a long and happy life together.

> OR you choose feelings ("while I feel love, I'll stay with you"), and your marriage is doomed.

> EITHER you choose gratitude toward your parental home, forgiveness, and care, and your life will be full of joy and blessings from your extended family.

> OR you choose "childhood traumas" when you view your parents as "toxic". Then, do not be surprised with problems in your personal life, self-perception, and future trajectory. Besides, if you make this 'trauma choice' your children will be deprived of the attention of grandparents who are ready to love them, and you will not receive the blessings of the extended family.

On the "Worst Childhood Trauma"

Childhood trauma specialists love to obsess over the belief "tragedy of an unwanted child."

Long-term observational studies confirm that children born of love and careful planning, often firstborns conceived after marriage, do tend to have greater confidence and success in life. That's a fact though there are exceptions.

It is not destiny. Choice matters, choice can change everything.

I've counseled many adults fixated on:

- *"My parents never wanted me."*

- *"They owe me an apology for ruining my life."*

- *"I'll only heal if they grovel and beg for my forgiveness."*

These "deeply traumatized individuals" were always surprised when I refused to work on this so-called trauma and blame their parents but I offer them to take responsibility for their adult life issues.

A Personal Story of Redemption

My husband's mother conceived him during a very difficult time in her life: an abusive alcoholic husband, lack of money, a struggling eldest son, problems at work. She planned to have an abortion.

That same day, her cousin aunt Dusya came over. When Dusya learnt what her cousin niece planned to do, she knelt in the doorway:

> *"Olga, I beg you! Keep this baby! I'll pray that he brings you joy and support. I'll help you raise him! Just let him live!"*

Thanks to Dusya, my husband was born.

He grew up knowing this story and adored Dusya, who called him *"the prayed-for child."* He never resented his mother for her initial hesitation. On the contrary, she became a cherished part of his life, a wonderful mother-in-law to me and a beloved grandmother to our kids.

It was at one of the workshops at the University where we studied psychology, my husband "got the truth" that "he had been living his whole life under the "burden of the worst of the childhood traumas destroying him from within and crippling his potential" 😊.

That's when we realized something crucial: **psychology has its nonsense peddlers, but they have nothing to do with classical science**; to recognize these peddlers and filter out their teachings is very important otherwise they will hurt us as psychologists and those who come for help.

Your personal choice matters!

Two Filters That Saved Us

People often ask how we (me and my husband – when he was alive) manage to stay grounded amid so much information.

Two things come to mind.

- First, we came to psychology already carrying the experience of overcoming crises, not only in our own lives, but also in the lives of other people who joined us on various marital gatherings. One of our university instructors once complimented us saying that only about five percent of people come into psychology not just to "figure themselves out," but with the desire to help people and to share knowledge and experience with others.

- Second, we came as believers, familiar with the Laws and principles given to humanity from Above. This always allowed us to immediately filter everything we heard through the lens of global ethical standards and decide what we would use in our practice and what we would reject as contradicting the laws of Goodness.

In Conclusion

In life, everything depends on making the choices including who you listen to, what you read, and what core values guide the way you live.

Wishing you wisdom and love, dear friends.

CHAPTER TWO

THE HEALING SANDWICH TECHNIQUE: TREATING RESENTMENT

I would like to present a method I call 'The Healing Sandwich'. To demonstrate how it works, I will share Anna's story with you.

Anna's Confession

"I'm 34. On the surface, my life looks perfect. I am in great shape. I am intelligent. I have a great career. I speak three languages. My own house in Sochi is just a fifteen-minute walk from the sea. I have an apartment in Moscow where I work, and I'm considering buying property in Europe. In short, I have everything but happiness. I know what's missing: a family. It's not that I lack attention from guys. That's never been a problem. But nothing lasts. I prefer to take relationships seriously. I won't settle for living together. Yet somehow, I keep getting entangled all the time with the wrong guys"

Guy # One: *ELVIN*

"I was twenty, a university student, when I fell for a foreigner from a wealthy family. To me, a young girl living in a dorm, his name alone sounded so exotic. His manners were impeccable; his generosity was unmatched. Fine dining? Only the best restaurants. When my mother got sick and needed a doctor, he (sparing no expense) found the top specialist. When I decided to rent my own apartment, he covered the cost of me living in a nice area. For almost two and a half years I lived safely "under his caring wings". After graduation, he returned to Azerbaijan (a country in the South of Eurasia), promising: 'I'll take care of everything and get it all organized for our future together.' For about a year, we emailed each other. Then he invited me to visit and said he missed me terribly. I took time off and flew to see him. He set me up in a beautiful apartment overlooking the sea. Everything was romantic. However, he wasn't in a rush to introduce me to his family. And then, one morning, after he left for work, there was a knock on the door.

It was his wife accompanied by a big muscular man, her elder brother. It turned out that she married Elvin six months before. His parents chose her as a bride for him several years ago. She was already pregnant and had some health issues with her pregnancy and that's why they did not have a sex life for several months, but they had a "solid" marriage, built on mutual respect, a shared family business, and the expectation of a son. I learned all of this from her own lips as she stood in my cozy little love nest.

I packed my bags quickly and left without hesitation as they handed me a pre-booked plane ticket and drove me to the airport.

I won't go into details about how later I shut down all Elvin's attempts to contact me...

Guy # Two: *GENE*

"I was twenty-seven, a successful manager at a prosperous company. Still dreaming of a family. He was a strong-silent type like a movie-cop: a tough guy of a few words, and very straightforward. We met at a corporate event. He oversaw security. On our second date, he took me to a restaurant and said: "I need you. I don't have time for romantic dramas. If you're ready for something serious, here I am." Our dates over those several months were mostly about having dinner together, two or three times a week, either at his place or mine; watching movies he found interesting; and him taking me to a New Year's corporate party at one of the companies where he was responsible for security. He would introduce me to everyone as "his special lady" (whatever it meant). Every time I asked questions about his family, his parents, his past he would either dodge my questions or shut me down with jokes like, "curiosity killed the cat" or he would simply say, "you'll know everything when the time's right". What did we talk about? About everything except the things that matter. But I was charmed by the way he talked about family in general, the human soul in general, and the society in general. He would tell me about his job, share memories from childhood, and listen to me with interest. There were a few red flags.

The most serious ones were his aggression and jealousy. If my opinion sharply clashed with him, he would raise his voice and argue. It would make me feel very naïve, silly, or uncomfortable to have an opinion. He always was alarmed about my phone calls, and wanted to know: "Who is it? What do they want?", and if it was a man, even if it was a colleague, boss, or a subordinate, he'd react with passive-aggressive comments like: "There are too many guys in your life, don't you think?" One day I made a comment jokingly, "I don't owe explanations to a man who isn't even my fiancé, don't you think?" His reaction was scary: he snatched the phone out of my hand mid-conversation, slammed it against the wall, and walked out. I was stunned. Then I pulled myself together, and I left. He caught up with me, started saying how much I meant to him, how amazing I was, and handed me a brand-new phone, the latest model, apparently a birthday gift he'd been saving for me. He joked: "That's why I smashed the old one, so you'd appreciate this one more!" And I melted.

But a week later, I got an email from somebody anonymous with videos of him with other women in very suggestive situations. When I confronted him, he said it was all fake, "someone's trying to sabotage me," and the videos were "from a past life." I said: "I don't even know what kind of past life you are talking about!". Suddenly it all came spilling out: how miserable he was with his first wife. I was stunned: he was married before? He said he needed to "blow off steam" with other women (more than one?), how his terrible ex-wife wouldn't let him see his kids. What? He has kids? He said his ex-wife remarried and now "her jerk" was raising his children, and how he was suing her for full custody "to teach her a lesson." That's when I realized I'd almost gotten trapped in a relationship with a monster. Before walking away for good, I found his ex-wife's contact info and called her, introduced myself, and heard her story. It was a story of physical and emotional abuse that lasted eleven years. It wasn't easy to end things with Gene. He didn't like to be the person who was left. It was a miracle that I got out of this relationship.

Guy # Three: STAN

"Stan. I probably would marry him. We've known each other for over five years, and we have been dating for more than a year. We're not living together, but everyone assumes we're a couple. He introduces me as 'his woman.' (What does that mean? Mistress? Escort? Lover?)

Whenever I ask, he shrugs it off: 'Don't rush things.'

Déjà vu, again

He filled my world and became an important part of my life. At work, we lead parallel project teams. In life, he fixes my flat tires, broken door locks, and even finds me the best cell plans. He's my shoulder to cry on, my friend to support me in a time of need. But he is not my fiancé as he hasn't proposed yet. When he's in the romantic mood, life is magical. He makes me feel like a queen for a day, a weekend, and a few days in a romantic getaway. He knows how to live big. I've come to realize he likes being a prince. Once, when I was frustrated, I blurted out, "Do you like pretending you are a prince?" He laughed and agreeingly tried turning everything into a joke. I stormed out, slamming the door in his office. That evening, he brought me flowers with promises of "forever together". He told me he couldn't imagine his life without me. And once again I melted.

Recently, I asked myself: "If Stan proposed to me, would I say yes?" And the answer I gave myself was: "I'm not sure. I'm scared". Deep down in my heart, I know I've stumbled into another empty illusion. Another round of loneliness. Void. That's why I came to you. A colleague at work spoke highly of you..."

Anna looked surprised when I began asking her about her family.

"You sound like a baby brought by a stork somewhere, "I said gently. "It's as if you erased the first twenty years of your life and the people in your family. You haven't mentioned the house where you were raised. Why?"

It turned out Anna had cut off all contact with her parents. Completely. Years ago, at the very start of her career, before *Elvin her First* broke her heart, she attended a training led by a certified specialist on "Freedom Oriented Life" That's where she first heard the term *"separation."* Over the next few months, she spent a lot of money on individual sessions to *"work on her inner child freedom"* and *"escape the dead ends created by her mother and father figures".* In a dramatic finale to these *"revelation"* sessions, Anna wrote her parents a farewell letter. In it, she told them that she was cutting them out of her life. She also *cut off her* sister as well. Why? Because during those sessions she had a *"clear realization"* that her sister had always been *"an anchor dragging her to the bottom."*

For years, Anna worked on creating this "Freedom Oriented Life" convincing herself she was happy *"living without anchors."* Occasionally, she heard news about her family, her sister, her mom, her nephew; and felt a desire to see them, maybe for her mother's birthday or New Year's family parties. But she would not go through with it, reminding herself that *"if she softened, she would let toxic past back in"*, the very past she had supposedly *"escaped from just in time."*

The hardest period came after Gene (*the Second*), when she sank into a deep depression. She was constantly tired with no energy to even make a cup of tea. She called in sick a lot and spent days in bed, chain-smoking, a habit she had not picked up since her college years. Suddenly she realized that something was off. She called her friend, a doctor, who admitted her to a clinic. There, she was diagnosed with akinesia among other things, a severe case of depression. She spent two weeks in treatment. When offered psychological counseling, Anna refused.

Now, as I asked about her family, Anna grew anxious: she thought I was about to drag her back into another endless cycle of "cutting off anchors." She burst out: "I already worked through all my childhood traumas eight years ago! My inner child is free from limiting thoughts and destructive behavior patterns! I'm sure the problem lies elsewhere."

"You're absolutely right," I reassured her calmly. "The problem *is* elsewhere. And no, I am not here to take you back to excavate your traumas."

Anna chuckled; the tension in her face softened.

"Your life," I continued, "is a tragic illustration of several old proverbs: *'Like attracts like.'* You are drawn to men who mirror your emotional state."

Anna looked at me, trying to grasp what I was saying.

"You are living trapped in many toxic emotions. It distorts your perception, making you view the world through the lens of resentment, shame, fear, and guilt. You cannot develop healthy relationships with men who have strong values. And you do not find these men attractive or appealing. They seem boring to you because you live in totally different worlds. And consciously or not, they keep their distance. As a result, you do not meet many of them in your every day life. When you carry around a heavy and bitter emotional load, you cannot come close to anyone who is free from that load. You crave intense emotions, unpredictable relationships, drama and excitement; you are *drawn* to these *'alpha males'*, these *tough-guy types,* and when you are with them, you lose touch with reality and lose yourself."

Silence. Anna was absorbing my words.

"Consider this your diagnosis," I said. "Now, it's your turn. What will you do with this information? You have two options:

> **Either** you keep living the same way, bouncing from one emotional storm to the next,

> **Or** you make a different choice based on different values."

I paused then went on saying, "I'll only work with you if you choose the second option. Stick with the first, and you'll have no trouble finding another specialist, but it will not be me."

"You know what? You're right," Anna said, looking at me with a reflective gaze. "About four years ago, when things with 'Number Three' were just starting, there was this guy who liked me and who by your definition, was a 'normal' one, with a good family, serious intentions, stable, kind, and reliable. But I instantly shut him down and told him, 'You're just not my type.' I mean, I did not feel the spark between us.

She paused, then added with a sadness:

"I hear, he turned out to be a great husband, and an amazing father. He is now the head of a business line in our company. And you're right again; his interest in me faded just as fast as it started. I guess he realized I was not a girl to have a future with."

"So, what is your choice now?"

"I want to work with you."

"Then we're going to work on transforming all the mess you created in your life."

"Transforming?" She asked, surprised. "Aren't we supposed to dig out the mess and dispose of it?"

"I used the word *"transform"* on purpose. That's exactly what we'll do. In fact, I used a gentle term, my husband puts it a bit more bluntly: 'We're going to turn your crap into fertilizer.'"

Anna burst out laughing. In that moment, this emotionally burdened and very reserved woman got transformed into a playful, lighthearted girl. It was as if she'd shaken off years of carrying and nursing her emotional burden.

"I love your husband's quote!" She laughed. "Yes, that's it! I don't have a 'situation' to unpack. My life is full of crap, and I am ready to get rid of it."

"No, we will not get rid of it", I corrected her again, "why waste what you've been collecting all these years? We're going to use all of it and turn it into fertilizer!"

Anna and the Healing Sandwich Technique

"I'm ready!'"

"Draw five columns on a piece of paper. Label the first one 'People'. Second: '+'. Third: '–'. In the fourth, draw a grumpy face ☹, and in the fifth, a heart ♡.

Let's start with your parents. Whose name are you going to put down first?"

Anna wrote "Dad", then corrected herself: "Father".

People	+	–	☹	♡
Father				

"Tell me about him," I suggested.

"The word 'father' brings nothing but awful memories. As a child, I waited to see what mood he was in when he came home. I had to wait, my sister waited, and so did my mom. Sometimes he came home happy and kind and we tried not to make him angry. Even when he was in a good mood and asked me something simple my inner radar would be fully on, trying to guess the 'right' answer not to rock the boat. Because if I didn't, it could switch instantly. As if

someone turned off the light switch, and we would be engulfed in a storm of yelling, fear and tension. Would he hit Mom? Would he rip the door off its hinges? Would he smash the teapot into the wall? Would he yank my sister by her shirt collar?

The strange thing is he never laid his finger on me. At least, I don't remember it. Mom told me once that when I was three or four, he raised his hand to hit me, and I screamed: 'I will tell Uncle Serge and he will put you in jail!' Uncle Serge was our neighbor, a police-man, who always gave me candy. When I yelled those words, my father stopped at once, laughed, and went to bed.

"Nevertheless, I saw him hit and push my mom and my sister. They always had bruises. Later, when I was 9 or 10, I started asking my mom to divorce him. But she never did. I moved away at the age of 17 to go to college. Mom resented me for 'abandoning' her, even though my sister was still there. My sister eventually got married, then she got divorced, her husband was worse than my dad. For a while they all lived together: my mom, my sister, my nephew, and my dad. His outbursts became rare but never disappeared completely. Mom continued to endure it all, while watching her grandson being raised in the same nightmare. Only many years later, during a legal matter with my grandma's estate, a lawyer advised her to file for divorce. My mom and sister finally moved out on their own. At last."

I raised my hand gently to interrupt Anna.

"Let's turn to our table. In the second column, the '+' is for good memories. Do you have any good memories about your dad?"

"No, I don't."

"That's impossible. Your brain holds plenty of good memories. That's how a child's mind works; it clings to the good. And those memories stay with us forever. For instance, your story about Uncle Serge counts. Your father listened to you, his little girl. Say it out loud first, then write it down."

Anna hesitated but finally said:

"Dad heard me, his four-year-old daughter, when I said I would tell on him to Uncle Serge"

She wrote it down. As she finished, her eyes lit up:

"You know what I just realized? *Thanks to dad, I'm very aware of any hint of abuse. Like an exposed wire, I sense it instantly."*

"Write that in the second column."

"And dad, despite all his issues, couldn't stand lies. His 'Don't lie!' still echoes in my head, along with: 'The worst thing is when people around you lie.' And: "Don't let anyone play you."

"Write: 'Thanks to dad, I can't tolerate lies.' And: 'Thanks to dad, I refuse mediocre relationships.'"

"All this, in the second column. All of it, thanks to dad." Anna's voice trembled with a mix of surprise and lingering pain at the revelations.

"Oh! I just remembered, every Saturday morning dad would go to the market, and he always used to take me with him. When I was little, I sat on his shoulders. Later, I held his hand. His hand was huge, rough, dry, but warm."

"Write it down."

"*And every time, he bought me cotton candy on a stick.*"

"Write that down too."

Eventually, I stopped Anna.

"Let's take a break here. It's time to start shaping the 'honey layers.'"

"Replace the '+' sign in the second column with: **'I thank you for...'**

People	Thank you for...	–	☹	♡
Father				

"Let's go. Make sure each 'layer' takes no more than ten seconds. I'll help you with the first one: 'Dad, I thank you for hearing me when I was four years old and threatened you with Uncle Sergei!' Say it after me."Anna fell silent.

"Repeat it."

"You don't understand." Her voice crackled with pain. "I can't. It feels like something in my head is shifting and moving inside me. It's unbearable!"

"Good," I said softly. "Then let's make sense of it all. Repeat after me..."

Anna went through each point in her "gratitude column". When she finished, she stared at me, stunned:

"It's like, like I'm sprouting wings!"

Then we moved on to the column marked with a "minus sign".

Here Anna had to write down all the painful memories she still carried about her dad. Again, each one was spoken out loud before being written down.

> *"Once I saw him shove Mom so hard she fell and started bleeding. I was so scared!"*

> *"I used to lie in bed and hear him cursing at my mom and it terrified me!"*

> *"He came home once from a parent-teacher meeting cursed and slapped my sister over something at school."*

> *"I remember him slamming the door and yelling: 'You're all three sluts!'. I cried the whole night."*

> *"Once he came home drunk and kicked us out of our house. It was cold and raining, and we had no coats or umbrellas. We went to my mom's friend's place, but nobody was home..."*

"Let's pause for a moment," I said gently. "It's time to prepare the next layer of our sandwich, the layer of bitter herbs."

"Will it hurt as much?"

"Yes."

Anna took a deep breath with her fists clenched.

"Now, in the third column, replace the minus sign with: **'It hurts me deeply when you…, but I forgive you.'**"

People	Thank you for...	It hurts me deeply when you…, but I forgive you	☹	♡
Father				

"Let's start. I can help you with the first one if you like."

"No," Anna said firmly.

She clenched her jaw, drew another deep breath, and said:

"I know how to do it now."

"Good. Say each item from your third column out loud, as if your father were sitting right here. Each one, ten seconds or less."

"Dad, it hurts me deeply when I remember you shoved mom and she fell and started bleeding. I was so scared. Years have passed, but I still remember."

I pointed to my watch as a gentle reminder to keep it brief.

"…But I forgive you."

She paused. Her face tensed, her voice was low and strained.

"But that's not true! It's a lie! Saying it doesn't mean I truly forgive him!"

"We'll talk more about what forgiveness truly is," I reassured her. "For now, you're learning to prepare 'the medicine' for your soul."

Anna continued, working through each memory in her third column. This time, she sounded more robotic than heartfelt; her emotions tangled in her voice, raw and unrestrained.

I asked, "Do you know the saying: 'A spoonful of honey helps the bitter medicine go down'?" Anna nodded.

"Bitter medicine is best swallowed quickly, and the most bitter ones are taken with sugar, jam, or honey, so their aftertaste doesn't linger. You tasted pure bitterness with this layer of forgiveness. Engrave this feeling in your memory, so you never again trap yourself in bitterness. Never use bitterness without honey of thankfulness and forgiveness"

"Okay. I'll remember." Relief flickered in Anna's voice.

"Let's keep going. Ready?"

"Yeah."

"In the fourth column, write down your dad's touchy subjects, the pain *you've* caused him or are still causing, anything you do now that could potentially hurt him. What does he expect from you but doesn't get?"

Anna snapped. Barely holding back her anger and frustration after what I said. She spoke. At first, her voice was low and slow, then it grew louder, faster, and more intense.

"I don't think I owe him anything! Why should I even care about *his* sore spots when he ruined my whole life? I can't build healthy relationships with men, because of him! I can't even look at my mother without feeling disappointed, because of him! I despise my sister for groveling to him over that apartment he deeded over to her, because of him! It's all because of him! I haven't seen him in over eight years, and I have no desire to!"

Anna's pain was pouring out of her. Her breathing quickened, her face flushed, her eyes flared with rage, and her voice crackled with hatred.

"Now it is time to go back to the third column," I said calmly, handing her the pen she had flung aside. "Write: *'He gave the apartment to my sister.'*"

She did that

"Now prepare this new much-needed bitter layer from that third column. Just like we practiced."

Anna bit her lip, then, through clenched teeth she pronounced slowly:

> *"Dad, you hurt me so much when you left the apartment for my sister instead of splitting it evenly between us. But I forgive you!"*

"Perfect. Now let's move on to the fourth column. I'll start summarizing your words, and you write them down:

> *"I do not think I owe anything to you.*
>
> *'I blamed you for my own failures with men.'*
>
> *'I haven't taken any attempts to see you in many years.'"*

Anna began writing, tapping the table impatiently with her pen cap.

"Now continue on your own," I encouraged.

She wrote:

'I don't call you, even though you've asked through friends and relatives.'
'I didn't wish you Happy 60th!'
'I exercised my right to your apartment'
Once, in anger, I told you I wished you were dead!'
I told you many times: "You are not a father to me." It was my favorite go-to response to anything you said since I was 17.'

"Let's pause here. Time for the next layer of our sandwich. Another honey layer, but this one is a different kind of honey. In the fourth column, replace the sad-face emoji with: **'And please forgive me for...'**"

People	Thank you for...	It hurts me deeply when you…, but I forgive you	And please forgive me for…	♡
Father				

"This is honey?" Anna asked skeptically.

"Yes. This is the sweetest kind of honey. It is freedom from guilt through acknowledgment of your own mistakes, even when you have spent years trying to justify yourself. Ready to make this layer? Or do you want my help?"

"I think I've got this," Anna said after a long breath. "I know how to follow the pattern."

She started calmly:

"Dad, please forgive me for thinking I owed you nothing."

"Dad, please forgive me for screaming in your face: 'You're not a father to me!'"

Each line was calm, clear, and deliberate. At one point her voice wavered, but then she inhaled, exhaled, and pulled herself together.

After the final sentence, she looked up expectantly. "What's next?"

"More honey, Anna! You can never have too much. Now write down what would *bless* your dad, what good, realistic things you *can* do for him. Things that would bring him joy. Write down these things in the last column"

Anna began writing:

"Call once a week." (My remark: "Be specific.")

"Tuesdays at 7 PM."

"When I visit during my vacation, take him to lunch at a café." (My remark: "When exactly?")

"Early June."

"Send him holiday cards"

"Once a month, order delivery of his favorite sushi rolls."

"And what should we name this fifth column?" Anna asked.

"Instead of the heart, write something strong and meaningful: **Blessing.** This is your decision to bring more honey into the world."

People	Thank you for…	It hurts me deeply when you…, but I forgive you	And please forgive me for…	Blessing
Father				

"Now, Anna, try to put together a Healing Sandwich. **Take one point from each column, link them into a flow, and say it all within 40 seconds or less, ten seconds each.**"

Anna took a deep breath and began:

> *"Dad, I thank you for teaching me not to lie. It saved me from unsatisfying relationships with Elvin and Gene and helped me notice red flags with Stan. But it still hurts so much, when I remember you calling my mom, sister, and me 'you sluts'. But I forgive you. And please forgive me for trying to erase you from my life, for never phoning you. Dad, every Thursday at 7 PM, I'll phone you, just to say, 'Hi, Dad. It's me.'"*

"Perfect! You nailed it in 30 seconds."

"But what will I talk about on Thursdays?"

"You don't need much. Start with 'Hi, Dad, it's me,' prepare a small healing sandwich of what to say in advance. Little bites each week will be enough to start your healing."

"It looks like little *canapés*!" Anna smiled.

"And remember this, my dear: the sandwiches (or *canapés*) aren't for your dad. **They're not meant to change him or magically fix your relationship.** Relationships take two people working together. These little 'sandwiches', these *canapés,* **are for YOU.**

> **You're the one** who will consume them, for bitter medicine is best taken with honey.

> **You're the one** cleaning your heart of poison: bitterness, resentment, fear, shame, guilt, and anger."

Fast forward eighteen months. Anna's story had become one of my "golden case studies." I still marvel at how wholeheartedly she threw herself into the healing process, how quickly she built her inner strength and took her life in a new direction. She restored her relationships with mom, sister, and father, first through telephone calls, later – visiting.

One afternoon, she called me, her voice radiant:

"I'm getting married!"

…Anthony was a widower with two young children, five-year-old Maria and three-year-old Victor. She met him at the funeral of his wife, who happened to be Anna's cousin on her mother's side. She'd never met Anthony before as Anna had spent eight years disconnected from her family. She looked a lot like her cousin, and on that tragic day, little Victor climbed into Anna's lap, clung to her, and whispered: "Mommy, don't leave us, okay?" Anna's heart melted.

Her aunt Victoria, her mom's sister, always loved Anna. After the funeral, she started messaging Anna, sending pictures of the kids, coming to Moscow and visiting Anna with the children. Anna started to spend more time in her hometown. Eventually, she bought an apartment there when her company opened a new branch in her hometown, and she was offered a manager's position.

Things started to unfold rapidly. She and Anthony kept in touch via video, first just about the kids. Little Victor started calling her "Mama Anya" on the very first day. Six months later, Anthony, who was not a tough-guy type, awkwardly confessed to Anna that after his wife's passing, he hadn't even considered another woman, but Anna melted both his heart and the hearts of his young children.

By that time, Anna easily broke up with the guy Number Three. The new Anna (the one "cured by the healing sandwiches") was not his cup of tea anymore. One day, she also made a Healing Sandwich about him. Putting everything in perspective, she told him: "Thank you, Stan, for five years of friendship and support. It hurts knowing you strung me along with vague promises of marriage, but I forgive you. Please forgive me for clinging to fantasies and playing your game. With an honest heart, I bless us for going our separate ways. The truth is, you're not my future husband, and I'm not your future wife." Anna admitted it stung a little, how quickly he let go and turned his attention to the boss's new secretary. But the Healing Sandwich did its job: she was free.

"And guess what?" She told me at the end of that phone call. "Turns out, I can't have children of my own."

At first, I was stunned, her voice sounded so joyful, the news seemed dissonant.

As if sensing my confusion, Anna continued:

"Remember what you said once to me? You said that life is unpredictable, but God is so loving, there will always be surprises. You told me that if I have the right attitude, even unpleasant surprises will bear good fruit. When Anthony proposed, a verse from the Psalms flashed in my mind: *'He settles the childless woman in her home as a joyful mother of children.' That's me!"*

The Healing Sandwich cures Resentment; it is a powerful tool for the soul recovery, especially when an individual is poisoned with toxic emotions. The spiritual principles of *Gratitude, Forgiveness,* and *Blessing,* they heal the soul.

Making and tasting these sandwiches is *your* own choice.

It is *your* responsibility, regardless of how others behave toward you.

Let me say it again: **there are some things you can't afford to get wrong.**

No letters, no texts, no DMs. The Sandwiches must be spoken aloud, in private, never sent.

The Healing Sandwich is supposed to help <u>its maker's soul</u> restore wholeness and harmony.

- The *only* motivation for you to make and eat this sandwich must be the desire **to heal *your heart.***

- Any other motivation makes the sandwich ineffective or even harmful.

- Before you make or especially eat the sandwich, check your heart and immediately dispose of the sandwich if any of the following motives are true:

    — to change someone else,

    — to fix the relationship,

— to prove your righteousness (to yourself or others).

Any of these wrong motives turn the Healing Sandwich into manipulation and it becomes poisonous:

- **"Changing someone else":** using any means to "mold" a person into what you want is manipulation, even if it's wrapped in a sweet bun.

- **"Fixing the relationship":** relationships are a mutual process; trying to "take everything into your own hands and force things onto the righteous path" is like the impossible task of playing God; it leads only to dead ends and disappointment.

- **"Proving your righteousness":** flashy "super-spirituality" is always out of place; it irritates and harms both yourself and the relationship.

In Conclusion

The Healing Sandwich frees you from toxic emotions; however, it will become poisonous if you are driven by false motives.

Wishing you wisdom and love, dear friends.

CHAPTER THREE

SINGLE-USE vs. MULTIPLE-USE SANDWICH

Veronica, 24

"I'm leaving my husband! He's such a mama's boy! I married him, not his mother! And honestly, I was young and stupid. I rushed into this marriage just to get away from my parents. My sister and I were raised with an iron fist: our schoolwork was monitored; we weren't allowed to stay out late. Once when my mom came home after a late shift around midnight, she woke me up and made me wash the dishes because it was my turn and I did not do it before going to bed! Can you believe that? Another time, my dad got back from a business trip and did the same thing to my sister, woke her up because she did not clean her shoes. That's the kind of home we grew up in.

So, I got married thinking I'd finally get to decide for myself what to clean and when, but now I have my husband with his quirks. Just the other day he asked, 'Why did you *decide to change the wallpaper? I don't see the need." But I do not need a reason to change the wallpaper in my apartment, do I? I may just feel like it.*

Then there was this time: 'Let's go see my parents at the cottage. Mom has been asking when we are coming". He misses his mom, ha-ha. Good for him. Why do we have to go, when I want us to spend the weekend doing something else? Several days ago, he came up with his big idea for winter vacation: 'Let's drop George, our 5-year-old son, off at Mom's and hit the slopes for the weekend!" His company happens to organize a trip for top employees and their wives. "Forget it!" – that's what I told him plenty of times, our son isn't going to my in-laws! She'll raise him to be just as spineless as her precious boy! And my husband's coworkers? They are useless. You cannot talk to them about anything. They don't even know the difference between Mozart and Beethoven! on top of it, my husband is lazy and does nothing around the house...

I raised my hand slightly to signal, *"That's enough."*

Then I asked:

"So, your 'wimp', is he, in fact, lazy and spineless?"

"I just told you, didn't I?"

"I heard you say he works for a good company, he is well-respected, and I bet he makes good money."

"What does money have to do with it?! I'm talking about his mother and how he keeps undermining me!"

"How, specifically, does he undermine you? Can you give me an example?"

"Three days ago, he reminded me of his mom turning 50. He and his siblings want to chip in to buy her a car. Nothing fancy, just something their parents can use for trips to the summer cottage, since their old car keeps breaking down. He asked if I'd be okay with it. I was speechless! I reminded him that I was planning to get a new car for myself. And what did he say? - 'Your car is only a year old. I know you want to upgrade. We'll do it next year for your 25th birthday.' What does *my* birthday have to do with it? I just don't get why our family must be all about *his* mom!"

"Tell me, does your son George enjoy being at his grandma's?"

"What does it matter if he *enjoys* it or not? She's not good for him. When once I stopped taking him over there, he started wetting the bed. That's normal to you?! A kid gets so attached to his grandma; he can't function without her? I told her: 'Thanks to *you*, my kid has *enuresis* now all because of you!'"

"And how did she react?"

"She did what she always does, ran to her husband, to her other kids, to *my* parents! Now they're all calling me, saying it's *my fault* the boy's wetting the bed! They assured me that I deprive my child of her love and it is stressful for George! Is that normal? Blaming *me*, his *mother*, for my child's enuresis?!"

"And how's your relationship with your own parents?"

"There *is* no relationship! Didn't I tell you what kind of childhood I had? I cut them off."

"And what about your sister? Does she also keep her distance from them because of this 'unbearable childhood'?"

"What does my sister have to do with anything? Are you even listening to me? She's always with them: holidays, family trips. It is my sister, her husband, their kids, and my parents are always together. They don't even invite me anymore!"

She sniffled, feeling offended.

"So, leaving you out is how they show you don't matter to them. You don't matter to your husband because he still loves his family, and you want to cut him off from that..."

"You've twisted everything! I thought you were a family therapist, but you......!"

Her outburst of anger gave her temporary relief from the venomous emotions she had been drowning in. Anger, like a drug, triggers a flood of neurotransmitters and delivers a high, which is a false sense of clarity.

I said, calmly:

"I'm not your psychologist."

That conversation happened back in the late '90s.

My rule is to take notes after every session so that when a client comes back, sometimes even years later, I can recall the details. I revisited this exchange nearly twenty years later, flipping through a worn notebook from 1999. It wasn't easy to find, and it took time. I had to do it a while back.

I was leading an education seminar on "Ethics in Family Life" for teachers at colleges.

During a break, a woman in her mid-forties approached me.

"Do you remember me?"

I usually answer such questions with a joke: "Refresh my failing memory!"

She laughed, complimented my teaching and then added, unexpectedly:

"I think about you a lot these days. I believe it was a divine providence that brought me to your seminar. I'm Veronica."

As soon as she began recalling the details of our old conversation, everything came back to me as vividly as if it was just yesterday, not two decades ago.

After her divorce, Veronica never remarried. She had relationships, but they always "unraveled" quickly (her own words). She now runs a business, a small private preschool. Her son George didn't have a steady job despite the education she provided for him. He refused to "work for peanuts" and preferred occasional gigs as a driver. He, his wife Laura, and their 4-year-old daughter Diana were all living in Veronica's three-bedroom apartment.

"I've poured so much into Diana since the day she was born!" Veronica said, her voice brimming with a mix of pride and pain. "I've taken her to the circus, the puppet theater... She's been coming with me to my preschool since she was two. She

loves it there; the kids adore her, the teachers spoil her, and of course, me, her grandma's always around.

But my daughter-in-law, Laura, has a terrible habit: whenever she and George have a fight, she packs up Diana and runs to her mother's place. She cuts off all contact with me and George. I tried telling her: 'Laura, dear, this is so bad for Diana, it's affecting her!' But she snaps back every time: 'What's worse is how your deadbeat son is affecting her!'" (Déjà vu…)

"The last time, I didn't see my granddaughter for seven weeks! I was so sad! I called Laura 'mother', we always kept in touch. She told me how Diana was doing, but she begged: not to tell Laura because she blows up every time she finds out, and my heart can't take the stress.'

And my son, ugh, that lazy, useless boy…"

"You mean George?" I asked gently.

"Well, who else?! He doesn't even care! His response is always, 'Good riddance, less drama in the house.' Then he takes off to his grandparents for a sauna day or a fishing trip. Just disappears!"

"Do I get it right; he has a good relationship with both sets of grandparents?"

"When he turned 11, my ex demanded that I let our son visit his grandparents. At first, I resisted, but then I thought, 'Whatever.' Besides, I was starting a new relationship at the time… George's grandparents have always adored him. And

*they adore Diana too. Even Laura takes Diana there some-
times for fresh air, peace and quiet. Even when she and George
are fighting."*

"And how often do you visit?"

*"My mother-in-law? - never, of course. Why would I?
Especially since my ex-husband and his new family visit there
all the time.*

"And what about visiting your own parents?"

*"Not often. My younger sister was always my parents' favor-
ite. And as they get older, they're becoming even more toxic,
always telling me how to live. I could teach them a thing or
two! I go rarely but if I hear Diana's visiting them, I rush over
immediately. Though my mother doesn't always tell me when
Diana's there. I feel so hurt when she does that."*

"Veronica, what's your question for me?"

*"How do I convince Laura to stop cutting me off from Diana?
I don't know what switched in her head last week, but she's
back now. Diana and I ran into each other's arms.". Her voice
trembled, and she pulled a tissue from her bag. "Things seem
calm between Laura and George for now, but I'm terrified, it
could all blow up again any day. Divorce has been mentioned
more than once this past year. Let them fight if they must, let
them divorce if they want, but why should Diana suffer? And
why should I?"*

Silence. Veronica cried softly. After a few minutes:

"Do you have any advice?"

"You can wait for seven years. When Diana turns 11, she'll be able to decide for herself, maybe even tell her mother she *wants* to visit you."

A pause. Veronica was battling with herself inside. At last, she said:

"I had a feeling our conversation would go in this direction. You're going to bring up what happened 20 years ago, aren't you? It's very unpleasant."

"You KNEW it would be unpleasant. And yet you came to me for counseling. Should I remind you that I'm not your psychologist?"

She started speaking with passion, despair, and pain in her voice:

"I remember. I remember everything you said.
You think I don't see the parallels, but I do.
You think I haven't seen any other therapists? I have.
You think I haven't *let go* of my inner 'ideal mother'? I have.
You think I haven't *released* my ex-husband from my mind? I have.
I know I am not easy to be around. I am clingy and very sensitive, and I ask a lot of others.
But I can't help it. That's how I love, I guess. I was raised this way. That is what my parents instilled in me and now it is part of who I am."

I lifted my hand softly to let her know she should stop.

Veronica got quiet. Then she went on:

"I heard you say at the seminar that blaming parents is a dead end. You said that life is all about choice. And yet, here I am. My life has been messy, but I am finally ready to clean it up. I messed things up—with my husband, his folks, my parents, my sister, my nephews… and now I'm doing the same with my son's family

(Veronica's voice faltered. She reached for another tissue.)

…And so, we started what Veronica herself would later call *"re-writing the script of her life."*

Veronica admitted that she was drawn to the theory of **Eric Berne, the founder of Transactional Analysis.** She read and reread his book *Games People Play* so many times, recognizing herself in many of its illustrations. Referring to Berne during our sessions helped her quickly and effectively start cleaning up what she called "the mess in her life."

For context: Berne's approach to psychology and psychotherapy was an attempt to combine concepts from both psychoanalysis and behavioral psychology. *Games People Play*, first published in the late 20th century, caused quite a stir. At first, Berne wasn't taken seriously; many dismissed him as a pop psychologist. But over time, transactional analysis (TA) earned its rightful place in therapeutic practice, as it aligned fully with the constructive principles of classical psychology.

Berne, a highly skilled practitioner and passionate researcher, built his work on the idea that every personality is made up of three parts (a concept inspired by Freud):

- the **Child** — impulsive, emotional, and reactive;

- the **Parent** — critical, rule-based, commanding;

- and the **Adult** — the rational mediator between the two.

He helped his clients analyze four key areas of their lives:

First, people learn to evaluate the weight of each part within them and answer the question: "What's going wrong that I keep repeating the same patterns?"

Veronica quickly recognized the dominance of her "Child"— an impulsive, reactive, and often hysterical part of herself.

Second, Berne teaches clients to recognize "transactions"—behavioral patterns in their interactions with others. It helps answering the question: "How exactly do I keep getting stuck in these situations I don't like?"

In all her communications, in family or professional settings, Veronica operated from her emotional state, reacting based on "like/dislike" rather than rational thought.

Third, through transaction analysis, Berne guides people in identifying their "psychological games"—manipulative, unhealthy patterns of interaction. For example:

- Someone resentful toward a specific person or group - plays *"If It Weren't for Him/You…"*

- Someone bitter toward society- plays *"The Victim*: *"What do you expect from someone like me in such a rotten system?"*

- Someone angry at fate - plays *"Why Does This Always Happen to Me?!"*

With Veronica, we "played" through these games at our sessions, traced them in her daily life, often laughed at their absurdity. It helped her realize how her emotional "Child" kept pulling her into destructive patterns.

Fourth, Berne insists that psychological help only works when an individual fully acknowledges their role in writing their own "life script," accepts responsibility, practices new behaviors, and finally breaks free from old, self-sabotaging patterns.

Fast-forward several months: Veronica sold her three-bedroom apartment, bought a one-bedroom apartment for herself and helped George and Laura with the rest of the money when they bought their own place. It turned out George wasn't the "lazy deadbeat" she had painted him to be; he'd been working remotely for his father's company all along. Laura, meanwhile, found out she was pregnant, and George advised he saved enough money to buy a home without needing an overwhelming mortgage. Veronica's decision to give them part of her apartment money came at just the right time.

Once Veronica began "clearing up the mess she had created," George and Laura enrolled in a 12-week marriage enrichment program that my husband and I offered to couples. There, they learned about the importance of maintaining healthy relationships with extended families. The danger of Veronica losing access to her dear Diana was gone. The Sandwich that heals resentment helped everyone involved and it is still doing its part...

I consider the Healing Sandwich a universal tool

You might call it a **technique** or a **framework** that works flawlessly across all areas of human connection:

- between parents and children of any age,

- between spouses, coworkers,

- employees and managers,

- between neighbors…

It helps you stay emotionally steady and restore your internal balance, no matter what's going on around you.

Why did I call this method a *"sandwich"*? - Because food is essential for physical life, and the ingredients of this sandwich—**gratitude, forgiveness, and blessing**—are just as essential for relationships.

The sandwich is meant as a tool for ongoing use in all living relationships

"Living" doesn't mean it is harmonious or pleasant. Relationships can be conflicted, tense, even toxic, or abusive. But if there's contact, whether with coworkers, neighbors (especially those with thin apartment walls), or family, those relationships are living.

Let me repeat: relationships can be healthy or unhealthy, conditionally healthy or critically sick, active or stuck in; they can be anything. But if both parents and children are alive, the parent-child relationship is active/living too.

The Sandwich needs to be constantly replenished. You always need to have some "honey" ready to soothe the pain you're about to voice. That is a simple fact: close relationships don't happen without pain, after all, we're *living* beings.

During our family seminars, my husband and I often used the illustration of hedgehogs: when they're apart, they freeze; when they snuggle together, they poke each other with their quills. Over time, they adjust to each other's presence; it gets warm without being painful. But every now and then, one hedgehog moves the wrong way, and the other gets pricked. That's life. The key is expressing your feelings of hurt before they harden into resentment. The Healing Sandwich can help you with that process

And always — *always* — think about the **honey first**!

Say:

> *"Thank you for…*
>
> *I was really hurt when you… but I forgive you.*
>
> *And please forgive me for…"*
>
> Then add a blessing

Several case-studies from my practice

Dad, in his dementia, suddenly cursed at his daughter out, the one caring for him.

The choice for the daughter:

> EITHER burst into tears: *"How could this happen?! Dad never spoke to me like that before! I was always his favorite little girl! And now he's unbearable…"* — and sink into toxic emotions, drowning in irritation and bitterness that will inevitably spill over onto your other relationships.
>
> OR: *«Dad, I'm so grateful to God for you, and for those childhood memories of us like picking cherries in the garden still makes me smile. Right now, Dad, it hurts so much when you spit those awful words at me, but I'm not angry. I forgive you. And please forgive me for losing my temper and slamming the door in frustration. Dad, I love you, and I won't stop caring for you."*

A daughter once again ignored the agreement to be home by 10 PM. Her mother's choice:

> EITHER scold her, or pretend it's not a big deal, or cry silently into her pillow…
>
> OR another option: "Sweetheart, *I'm grateful for the delicious coffee you made for all of us this morning. But it hurts me deeply when you ignore our agreement about curfew as it comes from our care for each other. I forgive you. And please forgive me for letting this slide too many times before. You consider yourself an adult, and at 18, you legally are, so I bless us with honesty in this house: if you want to remain a daughter within this system, you'll follow our rules. If the rules feel too restrictive, it's time for you to find your own place and build your own system."*

Single-use Sandwiches

These are Sandwiches you prepare once, for a very specific, exclusive purpose.

This practice is highly effective for releasing long-held resentments from relationships that are permanently over. For instance, in cases where the person is no longer alive, or simply no longer relevant to your present life (ex-husbands, ex-boyfriends, ex-friends…).

People often ask: *"Should I even dig up the past?"*

I introduced Anna (the Anna from Chapter 2) to a Single-use Sandwich when we spoke about the part of her life involving her exes.

"Life is unpredictable," I told her. "It's full of surprises to see if you learned your lessons. Imagine you're at a dinner party, and suddenly you find yourself at the same table with someone who once hurt you, betrayed you, slandered you, rejected you. And suddenly you start to feel off, you want to leave, to ignore your own plans and expectations for the event, because that person is there. If you follow your mood, it means you let resentment take control of your life and you're back in the 'mess.' You face a choice: <u>either</u> lose because your toxic emotions rule you <u>or</u> turn that bitterness into a fertilizer."

Anna prepared a Single-use Sandwich for each of her exes: Elvin, Gene, and Stan. She even made one for Elvin's wife:

"I'm grateful to you for opening my eyes that day. It hurt so much to see the contempt in your eyes, but I forgive you. And please forgive me for unknowingly becoming part of a love triangle. I wish you happiness."

Anna carefully followed all the rules of the sandwiches. **No letters, no texts, no DMs. Single-use sandwiches must be spoken aloud, in private, never sent.**

…When it came to Veronica's story, she also needed a one-time sandwich to finally close the chapter with her ex-husband. For years, she lived steeping in negative emotions: first being angry at him, then at her mother-in-law, later at herself, her son, and even her daughter-in-law. She realized that leaving that chapter unfinished was weighing her down and keeping her from moving forward. She managed to verbalize her pain; how much it hurt that he let her go when he finally had enough. She wrapped that pain in the honey of gratitude for his care and patience, admitted her own mistakes, and wished him happiness.

The Sandwiches she prepared for her former mother-in-law made it possible for Veronica to step into her house, pick up her granddaughter, and have a calm, friendly conversation.

The ones for her parents and sister helped her let go of her bitterness over family gatherings she wasn't invited to because of her bad temper. In time, she noticed she was being included once again in family get-togethers. And perhaps most astonishingly, the Sandwiches she made under the name "Laura" (her daughter-in-law) worked a quiet miracle: Laura started calling her *"Mama Veronica"*

Veronica started enjoying lots of active relationships using Sandwiches without fear or toxic emotions.

Let me share another story about a Single-use Healing Sandwich

This is the story of Helen and her son, Ivan.

"…Until the age of 13, my son Ivan didn't ask about his father. When he was little, I explained it to him once: "Sometimes in life, a dad isn't there but thank God you've got Grandpa!" And truly, Grandpa was like a dad with capital D for my son.

My father, what a man! He and my mom adored their grandson. Ivan spent nearly all his holidays and school breaks with them in a small town 100 km from our city. There he had friends, fishing trips, motor scooter races, Grandma and Grandpa's garden, and a giant old dog named Argo, his loyal pal, born the same year as Ivan. Everything seemed perfect, and then my son found out by chance that his biological father lives in our city. Ivan learnt that he had a space at the city market just a fifteen-minute walk from our home. "How is that even possible?!" I will always remember the way my son said this: half a question, half a statement, filled with pain, confusion, and disbelief. My heart clenched. I thought I already lived through the pain caused by my husband leaving me for another woman. I was seven months pregnant at the time. He just packed his things and threw them over his shoulder, saying, "I'm done with you. I'll send the money regularly. But from now on, my life is separate and you're not part of it." He finalized the divorce quickly using all his connections, kept his word by never appearing in our lives, but the money transfers always came on time and properly documented (probably it was his assurance that I wouldn't take him to court if I ever tried).

But the pain came back that day when my son discovered his father was alive, so close all these years, totally ignoring his son's existence. The decision of Ivan to meet his dad made my stomach turn. I tried to discourage him, "A father isn't the one who conceives you, but the one who raises you, - I said, - A biological father isn't always a real father!" I even borrowed your phrase, Nadezhda, calling him a "sperm bank." But my son is firm: "Mom, don't stop me. I need to look him in the eyes."

I don't know how to handle it..."

Helen was doing her best to stay composed, but her voice trembled.

"Stay calm," I told her. "Adolescence is the age of choosing the values that shape a person's life. From what you've shared I see that your family has already instilled the right values in Ivan, a balanced sense of responsibility and integrity as a man. That's exactly why this news has shaken him so deeply; it doesn't fit the moral framework he's been raised with. You should support him in strengthening that framework. Don't discourage him."

"But what if it hurts him? I don't want him to experience rejection the way I did."

"Your son has received so much acceptance, love, care, and moral guidance in your family that any pain he faces now has the potential to make him stronger. He's standing at a crossroads where he can either learn forgiveness and blessing or fall prey toxic emotions like bitterness, fear, shame, and resentment. This is his chance to learn and pass the test. But he needs help in preparation for it."

That conversation happened during the summer family camp where I was leading educational sessions. The program was full of bonding activities and interactive seminars for both parents and teens. That same day I conducted a workshop with the teens called "You and Your Parents," where we talked about not just parental duties but also children's responsibilities (starting especially at the age around eleven). I shared the Healing Sandwich method at that workshop with the teens who were attending.

A boy approached me after the workshop was over.

"I saw you talking with my mom. I'm guessing it was about my dad and I?"

He asked directly, without beating around the bush, very maturely.

"Good guess." I replied.

"You don't mind me meeting", he paused, "that man?"

"If you mean your biological father, I support your decision"

"That's what I figured from today's workshop: thank, forgive, and let go."

"Yes. It heals you if you're going into that meeting with no illusions about a touching reunion or an outpouring of love from your biological father. You are not going to prove anything to him and do not accuse him of anything. You are going <u>to heal yourself</u> and let go of the rejection weighing you down."

"I have already prepared my Healing Sandwich. Can I share it with you?" He asked.

I nodded with a smile. The boy read the following:

'Dad, thank you for bringing me into this world. It hurts that you had erased me from your life immediately; Mom and I forgive you. Be happy, if you can!'"

"Drop the 'if you can', drop 'mom', because you do only your part. What you prepared is excellent!"

"Got it…" He smiled. "I have a request: Mom said she wants to come with me. But I would rather go alone. Please talk to her."

"Okay. I will." I told him.

A few days after I returned from that camp, Helen called me.

"I promised my son I wouldn't go with him. But I couldn't hold back and followed him quietly. I watched him walk into his father's shop. I saw through the big window how this man was working on some documents. He glanced at my boy and listened to him. There was no emotion on his face or maybe I just didn't notice? Ivan turned around and left. The man kept working on his papers. And you know what? I did something I didn't expect from myself. After Ivan disappeared around the corner I went inside the same shop. My ex looked up and recognized me right away. His face showed a lot: annoyance, fear, and defensiveness. I spoke. 'Alex, I'm grateful to you for my son. I realize how much pain you caused me, and the wound of disappointment and rejection still hasn't healed. But today, I forgive you. Please forgive me for only saying this now, after all these years of waiting for something. I truly bless you and myself with complete honesty. You are dead to me as a husband, as an ex-husband once and forever. Be happy!'"

I struggled to say the last words but managed to keep my voice steady. I was about to leave when I heard something behind me. He caught up with me, spun me around, and hissed in my ear:

"What have you done to me here? You sent the boy after me?"

"Hands off, please!" I never thought I could react to his touch as something alien, repulsive and unacceptable so quickly. My voice carried so much outrage that a nearby security guard rushed to help me. Alex lifted his hands, signaling to the security guard that everything was fine. I left his shop, and I realized that I lived for thirteen years in prison of unforgiveness. Now I am free."

Carl Rogers, a leading figure of the humanistic approach in psychology and the developer of the client-centered therapy method, argued that every person has an innate tendency to develop their potential. In other words, every human is individually designed to grow and improve. The role of a psychologist, an educator, a social worker, and any professional helping people achieve subjective well-being, is not to focus on the person's problems, but on the person themselves to activate these natural tendencies.

According to Rogers, problems arise when the discrepancy between the "real self" and the "ideal self" reaches a critical level. The "real self" is the person's perception of themselves based on phenomenological experience with the external world, while the "ideal self" is the image a person holds of their perfect self. It is important to bring these two selves closer by lowering unrealistic demands on the "ideal self" while simultaneously expanding the possibilities of the "real self" through developing self-respect, self-expression, and self-disclosure in how we relate to ourselves and those around us.

For Ivan, there had been a breakdown between his real self (*"I've been erased by my father"*) and his ideal self (*"Am I loved or rejected? Am I strong or weak?"*). His decision to meet his biological father, tell him how he felt, forgive and release him, through Rogers' lens would be viewed as a clear activation of Ivan's inner desire toward personal wholeness. The same was true for Helen when she used the Healing Sandwich technique while speaking to her ex.

The need for love and belonging is at the core of what it means to be a human.

Abraham Maslow, the founder of self-actualization psychology, identified it (the need for love and belonging) as a vital tier in his world-famous *Hierarchy of Needs*. This need sits between both the physiological and the safety needs and the higher needs for esteem and self-actualization. Maslow believed that all people have both the desire and the potential to reach the pinnacle of the pyramid —self-actualization—across diverse dimensions of life, including psychological growth and the search for meaning. However, not everyone fulfills these "obligations to themselves."

Maslow listed several characteristics of a person who has potential to reach the highest level of the pyramid:

- a sense of belonging and unity with others;

- an ability to discern between instrumental means and ultimate ends;

- a clear sense of good and evil;

- and a democratic character structure (e.g., *"If I succeeded, so can others," "I can make mistakes, and so can others"* …)

Ivan by choosing a healthy attitude toward people including his father, who had disappeared from his life, rose above his disappointment and bitterness. When he acknowledged his feelings and offered forgiveness to this man, Ivan not only freed himself to move forward unburdened but also offered his father a glimpse of a path toward the release of toxic emotions, as a chance for his own redemption.

"How do you know that Alex wants to free himself from guilt?" Helen asked me this while we discussed the Healing Sandwiches that she and her son had prepared for tasting and replenishment.

"I don't know for sure, but there is a high likelihood," I replied. "In over thirty years of my practice experience, I have often met many 'Alexes' like him. I have seen any exceptions very seldom.

The past, unforgiven and uncovered, holds a person back, no matter how much they or those around them deny it."

In Conclusion

The past no longer exists. The future isn't here yet. But the present is a powerful resource for reflecting and re-evaluating the past, transforming your decisions, laying the groundwork for constructive steps into tomorrow.

Wishing you wisdom and love, dear readers.

Chapter Four

ADULT CHILDREN AND THEIR PARENTS. PARABLE OF THE PRODIGAL SON. VALLEY OF SORROW

Once there lived a man who had two sons. One day, the younger son decided that he was ready to be on his own, that his father's house with all its traditions and rules, was too small for his ambitions and that it was time to define life on his own terms. But there was a catch: he never accomplished or built anything in his life. He lived comfortably enjoying all the benefits of his father's house. Yet, he decided to ask his father for his portion of his father's inheritance. Harshly he demanded his father to give him his share of the future inheritance.

His son's insensitive demand broke the father's heart as he realized that this was not a passing whim of his son's youth but a conscious decision to distance himself from his family and family values. The father realized that if he did not allow his son to leave, the entire household would suffer under the boy's rebellion. The father could still hope that the boy wanted to invest in a good venture and find his footing outside the family home. Parents hope for the best for their children.

Within days, the young man took all his money and left. He abandoned his house and the town where he lived for a long time. He traveled far away, to ensure his "old folks" couldn't interfere in his life. Finally, he was his own master! There was nobody to tell him what to do! He had money, freedom, and opportunities. He was free to live as he pleased, indulging his every whim. Life was good, but his appetites were not being satisfied. His desires were empty and soon his funds ran out. To make things worse, a severe economic downturn struck that country. Famine, poverty, chaos, it all hit him like a tidal wave. He became so poor that he was desperate to do any work. Yet, the only work he could find was tending pigs. He found himself eating from the pigs' trough to survive. He felt lucky if there were scraps left for him after the pigs were done eating.

And then, one day, sitting there by the trough, watching the pigs devour their food, he came to his senses. He found himself as if someone else was living in his body before: foolish, short-sighted, harsh and dismissive of those who loved him.

At such a moment, you come back into your body and cast out the fool who had taken control with your permission. And you become yourself again.

That's exactly what happened to this young man.

What if he sought a guru on digging wounds…

Let's imagine their conversation:

"Tell me, wise guru, what's wrong with me? Why am I here, feeding pigs?"

"Well, you probably grew up in a hyper-controlling environment."

"What's that?"

"It's when you're smothered by too much care."

"Hmm… My father loved me and always protected me"

"Exactly. Classic hyper-control."

"I guess… yes, my dad cared a lot about me and my older brother preparing us for the future."

"Ah, so there's a brother? That's a textbook sibling rivalry situation."

"Sibling rivalry?"

"Sure, constant competition for father's love. That's a trauma your inner child never recovered from."

"Dad scolded us and disciplined us when we fought. He'd say brothers should look after one another"

"Whoa. Emotional abuse alert! A toxic father enforcing values and standards. You're clearly the product of that trauma. Tell me, was your mother on your brother's side too?"

"I don't really remember my mom."

"Oh no. Another layer of trauma! When she died you never filled the void and felt abandoned by her. Your father over-compensated with suffocating care for your mother's absence for your life due to her death. See? Parental control and selfishness disguised as love turned you into a codependent personality."

"But I asked Dad for my share of inheritance, so I could be independent, and he gave it to me."

"He provided for you and then allowed you to leave. Abandonment! Another deep wound" …

I will stop here. I will not go on modeling such nonsense. Sadly enough, this is the kind of nonsense that sometimes pours out behind closed doors in sessions with some specialists.

And what do you think happens next after such "treatment sessions"?

Psychological well-being? – No. Just deeper drowning in the poison of resentment.

A desire to restore relationships? – No. Instead, an obsession with grudges.

A move from the pig through to prosperity? – No. But a deep-rooted belief that only the session with the specialist can help you to get rid of disappointment.

The messages of the guru are the following:

"We've found someone to blame, and it is your mother and father while you stay pure and innocent at heart."

"The supposed silver lining is identified with the help of forced optimism. Start believing that "It is not as bad as that!" "At least, you are free, have boundaries, and have your own opinion!"

There is a plan to "expose father." He owes you for bringing you into this world, because you did not ask him to do that.

Such a scenario in the prodigal son's life after "coming to his senses" would be quite likely nowadays, when the teaching about childhood trauma and total parental responsibility for the fate of adult children became a pandemic-scale phenomenon.

The parable I'm referring to has a different turn of events.

… The young man came to his senses and said to himself, «What am I doing here? Back at my father's house, I saw when I was a kid that even the hired helpers had plenty of food. And here I am starving to death near a pig trough, not even allowed to eat my fill of the pigs' feed!"

He rose quickly and started his journey home: "Enough of this life!" He told himself, bolstering his resolve despite the shame, fear, and doubts gnawing at him. "I was disrespectful toward my father. I'm no longer worthy to be called his son. But maybe I can beg him to hire me as a servant. I won't demand anything. Never again! I'll tell him: 'Father, I have sinned against heaven and against you. I'm no longer worthy to be called your son; treat me as one of your hired hands.'"

It was a long journey back home, after all he had fled to a faraway land. Nevertheless, he continued toward his father's house with a repentant heart.

The father saw him from afar. He saw the sorry state his son was in. The father's heart stirred. He ran towards his son. Reaching him, he threw his arms around him and kissed him. People gathered; the workers of the father watched the return of the prodigal son. The father's kisses were the last thing the young man expected. Wrapped in his father's embrace, he told his father what he planned to say: "Father, I have sinned against heaven and against you. I'm no longer worthy to be called your son..."

But the father didn't let him finish. Turning to his servants, he exclaimed: «Bring the best robe! Please help him get dressed! Put a ring on his finger and sandals on his feet!»

The father would accept nothing less than a full reconciliation, not as a hired worker, but as his son. This return was too monumental to be celebrated by just a simple family meal. The father called for a feast: «Let's eat and celebrate! For this son of mine was dead and now he is alive again; he was lost and now he is found!"

And they began to feast.

This Gospel parable is known in Russian as "The Parable of the Prodigal Son," but in many English translations and other languages it's often referred to "The Parable of the Lost Son."

All those months (or years), this father had been mourning his lost son.

- *He didn't chase him down with lectures when the boy was living sinfully.*

- *He didn't take him to court to prevent him from losing all the inheritance.*

- *He didn't try to advise him on better investments.*

- *He didn't search for him to give him more money when he hit the rock bottom at the pig trough…*

He mourned him.

He mourned as one mourns someone who has made a self-destructive choice. For the father, his son was as good as dead, totally lost.

But now, the son has been found!

It is important to take into account that the son *found himself*, not *was found by someone*.

That is a very crucial detail in this story.

When a valuable coin rolls into a dark corner, someone looks for it.

Also, you must search for a foolish sheep that has wandered into a thicket.

But with a human being and their *deliberate* choice, the situation is different. In most cases people do not *accidentally"* slip into destructive behavior or *absentmindedly* wander into the thicket of hatred and disdain for values. By the age of 12 and beyond, it starts to be a conscious choice. There is no point in forcing anyone to come back to their senses if they don't want to. If you do, you will be blamed for "doing good," and get smeared with dirt.

That's why the father did not go searching for his dead/lost/prodigal son. He knew that his son's return is only possible by a MIRACLE, if the prodigal son HIMSELF wants to be found.

In most cases, such an awakening happens when a person hits their own "pig trough." And once they *"come to their senses"* they may choose repentance and moral values:

— for an addict vice, they must exchange the value of drugs for the value of life,

— for an abuser, the value of domination must give way to the value of relationships,

— for an adult child raging against their parents, the value of resentment and anger must be replaced with the value of a family bond,

— for parents, drowning in sorrow over prodigal adult children, the value of grief must shift toward the joy of connection with those children and grandchildren who want their love.

Galina's story

Galina attended a seminar on parent-child relationships where I was a speaker. During lunch, she sat at the same table as me and shared her story.

"We raised our kids the best we could. It was very hard during an economic crisis, my husband's factory shut down, my small teacher's salary barely kept us afloat. Friends helped us get into business, back then it was called 'shuttle trading.' We'd go abroad for goods, sell them for profit at the local market, then hit the road again. Meanwhile, our kids stayed with my parents. They're wonderful people, but of course children need their mom and dad. My husband and I did what we could when we were home: we spent time with our children, took them to the new entertainment centers, went on family trips, enrolled them in good schools…

Problems in our relationship started when our eldest daughter decided to study psychology at the University and we were bombarded with the endless talks about childhood trauma, lack of parental love, wounded inner child, and the emotional support she didn't get from her family home.

One evening at dinner my husband couldn't take her lectures anymore. 'Enough of this! You became too smart to start blaming and lecturing your parents?!'

She shot back: 'That's your unseparated inner boy talking, still clinging to your wife's parents and too afraid to take responsibility for your own life!'

That's when my husband said sharply: 'Out! Leave the table!'

She got up and announced: 'I've been meaning to separate from you. You are toxic parents, who do nothing but harming their children!' She slammed the door and left.

The fight was ugly. My husband gave her an ultimatum: apologize for disgraceful behavior or move out within three days. She left that night.

My husband was attacked on all the fronts. First, he was accused by me of 'not keeping his cool', and 'how important it was to show empathy for her youth'. Then my mother called him, furious that our daughter did not return home by morning. It turned out that our daughter was staying at her friends.

Now I see my husband was right all along. By the way, that night, when our daughter slammed the door, our younger kids surprised us with their support.

Our 16-year-old son said:

'Finally! Dad, I've been waiting for you to shut down her drama. How much longer were we supposed to put up with this?'

Our 13-year-old daughter asked:

'Dad, you're not going to chicken out, are you?'

'What do you mean?' My husband and I asked in unison.

'In three days, you're supposed to pay her next semester's tuition at the University. Are you seriously still going to do that after all this?'

Our son joked:

'Well, she does not find it revolting to take money from toxic parents who scarred her poor inner child. Gross! Your money is tainted!'- he mimicked her disdainful tone perfectly.

We burst out laughing, breaking the tension.

The eldest daughter came back home two days later, refusing to talk to us or sit at our table. She bought some ready-made meals with money her loving grandmother gave her. On the third day, silently, she placed her university bill on the table showing the amount due.

My husband placed a prepared list of her share of the household utility bills and rent on top of her university statement.

"And what's this?" For the first time in a few days, the daughter spoke to her father. She tried to speak with a condescending, dismissive tone though her eyes darted nervously.

"This is what you owe us. You decided to be the renter in our own apartment. I'm taking this game seriously. You have a small choice. Either you're a tenant, in which case you have no rights to our fridge or our wallet, and I'll add rent charges to this bill. Or you're our daughter, and then you have the right to be a part of our family, enjoy its benefits, follow its rules and contribute by doing your share around the house. Either way, this game ends here."

I won't repeat all the awful things our daughter screamed at my husband and me, at her smirking brother, and at her youngest sister who was giggling at the scene. The eldest slammed doors packed some things, and after about fifteen minutes rushed out of the house with a backpack and a laptop. Half an hour later my mother called, her voice outraged, demanding an explanation. My daughter went to her house and talked about her "toxic" parents in vivid colors. But by then, I already spoke to my father about what had happened, and our daughter found no more "receptive ears" in my parents.

Meanwhile, we were waiting at home for more drama to unfold. I was so surprised when my husband told me at that moment that he had been following your blog for several weeks.

"You hate psychologists!" I exclaimed then, and he replied, "As it turned out, not all of them".

It was your blog that helped me support my husband during that difficult time with our daughter, not to give in and to keep my sanity. I was reflecting on my inner self for weeks before that event, wondering where I went wrong with our daughter, trying to figure out how to reach her. In your blog I read about how unacceptable it is for adult children to be rude especially when they are living off their parents within their system; about the importance of forgiving children; and that forgiveness and mutual relationships don't always go hand in hand. I understood that it is possible to continue building relationships and financially supporting children ONLY AFTER their repentance, which means a real change in behavior which stops parasitic relationships with the family and blaming- parents attitude.

My daughter came home. She "put on a face." She apologized. The rude outbursts stopped. She began to behave properly. She asked for a list of her chores. She stuck to it: cooked dinner three times a week, did the dishes on Tuesdays and Fridays. Recently, I accidentally saw her in your account!!! I could tell by her face she didn't like what she was reading and listening but she WAS READING and LISTENING.

One day my daughter asked:

"Mom, if I had left for good back then and cut off all contact with you and Dad and erased you from my life, would you really have considered me lost? Or dead, like in that parable of the prodigal son?"

Her question came out, in a voice that carried a tone I hadn't heard in years, very soft and human. I felt the tears rising but I remained composed and answered her question with a question: "Would I have a choice?"

She was quiet for a moment, then asked:

"So you wouldn't have come looking for me? You wouldn't have begged for my forgiveness over all the things I accused you and Dad of?"

"Would that have changed your heart?"

"No," my daughter admitted. "I loved blaming you both for everything. I really believed all that crap back then."

And suddenly she threw her arms around me, and we both started crying.

"Mom, you and Dad would have had to walk through the Valley of Sorrow, and now I can see how hard it's been for you with me." "No, sweetheart. It's not being with you that was hard, it's the waiting. Waiting to see what choice you'll make next. Because that choice determines whether we must enter the valley of sorrow or not."

To make the long story short, now our daughter is no longer an A-student, because she became a fierce debater at seminars with some University teachers. But my husband and I are glad. Somehow, now when she's getting Cs for some of her courses, like "parents-to-blame", we're confident she'll make a decent psychologist...

In Galina's story, there's a happy ending. But unfortunately, not every family gets one. Many parents go through the Valley of Sorrow because not every "prodigal child" comes to their senses and undergoes that beautiful transformation of "being dead and then alive again, lost and then found." Some spend decades, even their entire lives at the "pig trough," drowning in their own misinformation as "luckily separated" children who place a lot of emotional and practical demands on their parents.

Parents whose child is "lost," or "prodigal" enter the Valley of Sorrow. Grieving follows its own laws, no matter what loss a person faces: loss of property, loss of job, divorce, death of a spouse, or a "prodigal adult child."

There are many theories about grief, but they all agree that grieving is a process which has stages. The number of stages may vary from theory to theory, but the core remains the same. Until all stages of grief are passed, a person cannot live fully.

Let's look at these stages in the Valley of Sorrow focusing on parents of "prodigal" children.

Stage One: DENIAL

This stage often takes three forms:

- **Denial of the prodigal's choice to estrange the loved ones and challenges to find justification to the behavior:**

  "No, no! It can't be that my boy, always so attentive and loving, refused to come to Dad's birthday! It must be his wife's doing, she never wants to visit us!"

  "My daughter is just searching for herself, she works a lot, she's upset because of the divorce, she doesn't want to upset us, that's why she doesn't call or visit, that is the reason why she didn't come to the hospital after Mom's surgery..."

Justifying the behavior of the prodigal children or trying to logically explain their behavior as due to circumstances or someone's influence is a dead-end and a self-deceptive concept. The intentional disregard for your family traditions is a conscious choice for the grown child to "die for the parents" or to "get lost for the family". It doesn't matter what motivates this choice: the mood of the spouse, visits to a "childhood trauma" specialist, or unwillingness to waste time on "stupid visits".

- **Trying to strike a deal**

> *"If it's so important for our daughter/son, let us admit that we were "toxic" parents, who did not give enough love, who disciplined, or who neglected the child's sensitive soul, well, okay, we'll do that for the sake of the relationship and everyone's wellbeing"*

> *"We will listen to our grown child and speak carefully not to upset him or her, go only where they recommend us to go, play only the games they allow, wear only the clothes they approve of, and give them as much money as they ask for..."*

This kind of deal is like opening a Pandora's box: once you agree to one issue, they'll remind you of hundreds more; once you make one concession, thousands of other demands and complaints will pour down on you. No negotiation tables work here. It is a matter of their choice, and it has nothing to do with parents' mistakes.

There are voices suggesting you should find a specialist who can help both sides 'make a deal.' But the problem is, a negotiation table implies a conversation between equals. But it's impossible to make parents and children equal in terms of family hierarchy. Just like it's ineffective to use a negotiations table for a supervisor and a subordinate or a mentor and a mentee.

For lovers of "democratic family relationships" I say that even in the most democratic societies there is a hierarchy of relationships and a division of responsibility according to tasks and goals at each stage. Relationships with parents are a matter of willingness to relate. Generally, parents are willing to have relationships with their children and in most cases, when I talk to parents of "prodigal children" I see this clearly. But as for the "prodigal children," they usually are not interested in relationships with their parents. They find satisfaction in playing blame games:

'you are no longer parents to me because I'm an adult';

'you must listen and agree with me, or you won't see me or your grandchildren';

'I see your effort to make peace with me as a violation of my boundaries and a threat to my separation process';

'I owe you nothing, but you owe me everything because: "I didn't ask you to bring me into this world."

Right now, these ideas based on "I didn't ask you to have me" or "you had me because of your own decisions and lust, so now you have to do everything for me!" - are very popular. At any rate, there is nothing new under the sun. Three thousand years ago, the prophet Isaiah rebuked such people:

"Woe to him who quarrels with his Maker, a potsherd among potsherds! Woe to him who says to his father, 'What are you begetting?' or to his mother, 'What have you brought forth?'"

A sinful attitude and demands toward parents and God bring sorrow. These people bring sorrow upon themselves and their children, they act from fear, resentment, and disappointment very often they are part of the childfree movement.

I tell such adult children directly to get off the needle of demands towards parents!

I tell these parents to stop feeding children nonsense like, "I had you so you would bring joy into my life!" or "You are my happiness, and you owe me nothing!" Children are not hamsters or puppies that you get for your own pleasure or comfort. Children are not your creation. Life is in the hands of the Creator, and its beginning is not just a simple biological union of two cells.

- **Downplaying the loss – another form of denial stage**

Parents live pretending their child's behavior doesn't affect them. They throw themselves into work, friendships, other children (if they have any), start new life projects, or sometimes drown their grief in various addictions such as binge-watching series, alcohol, or gadgets. These distractions act like painkillers, dulling emotional pain. But painkillers don't heal. They numb the suffering, while the process of emotional decay continues and erupts either into depression or psychosomatic illnesses. When stuck in this stage, instead of properly going through the Valley of Sorrow, parents prefer convincing themselves and others that "everything is fine," and 'with time, things will settle and normalize on their own'. It is a form of self-deception.

Sometimes parents stay in denial for years:

- they try to break through the wall of alienation, hatred, anger, and accusations built by their prodigal child;

- they close their eyes to the obvious: this child cut ties with them, choosing "traumas," resentments, and ambitions over a relationship. There's nothing parents can do here. The sooner parents move through the denial stage; the sooner they will have a chance to be healed.

Dear parents of prodigal children, it's important to acknowledge:

What's happening is awfully painful;

Your adult child deliberately causes you pain, so it is not your fault but it is their decision;

Your healing and recovering are your responsibility;

This terrible catastrophe did happen to you. Do not ignore the fact. Sadly, this catastrophe is universal.

Stage Two: ANGER TURNED INWARD

Sometimes this stage overlaps with the first stage, starting there and then continuing further. There are two main paths during this stage of the Valley of Sorrow.

The path of self-examination and self-blame searching for the reason why your adult son or daughter, once your sweet little kid, behaves the way they do now. This is rather pointless because:

first, "there is no one righteous" everyone makes mistakes; what is happening in the lives of all adults is a matter of their choice, but not their parents;

second, the "childhood trauma" theory has gone beyond reason; today it serves as a bottomless money pit for specialists who happily dissect your wounds and unpack your "traumas". This process can become never-ending.

third, toxic emotions (guilt, fear, resentment, shame) trigger a strong surge of neurotransmitters in the brain, acting as a powerful painkiller. It activates the "Bruce Almighty syndrome": the sweet feeling of one's own superiority, where one thinks "I hold the entire process in the palm of my hand, and I can mold another person to fit my expectations."

Wake up, dear parents! Don't take too much! The life of your adult child is their own. Not yours. There are no perfect parents. You gave your children what you could, and now they are living their own individual lives. Stop seeing yourself as the "creator of the universe". Stop thinking that you can make any person to live the way you want them to live.

The saying "you reap what you sow" is well known. But when it comes to people, it doesn't work the same way as it does in agriculture. Even perfect parents who sowed only wheat cannot control weeds which grow alongside. Adult children decide what they will cultivate: wheat or weeds. Their decision correlates with their choice, not with their parents or whoever.

I will use my husband's quote again: "Everyone has crap in their life. And that's okay. There is a choice to turn it into fertilizer. And there is another choice - to stay stuck in all the crap."

You cannot make decisions for another person (even if this person is your own child). However, you can make one for yourself:

EITHER "I refuse to stay stuck in this unpleasant mess. And if my grown child chooses to live there, I do not have to join."

OR "I like staying stuck in the crap"

The path of spiritual disappointment and "righteous self-torment":

"This is my punishment, my karma, the boomerang for how I treated my own parents, for straying away from God in my youth, for not praying enough for this child, for not having enough faith..."

Our lives are not solely (or even primarily) shaped by our parents or our genetics. The course of human life depends directly on the *values* that a person chooses.

"See, I have set before you today **a blessing and a curse...**", the choice is definite from Above to each of us.

Blessing lies in repentance, forgiveness, gratitude, mercy, love, and resisting evil. And it's *never* too late to choose it, at any point in life.

Curse lies in aggression, pretenses, resentment, shame, and guilt when people choose those destructive emotions, and they can make it at any age (unfortunately).

The Healing Sandwich can be a choice of blessing toward an adult child from mother and father:

"My son/daughter, I **thank** God that He gave you not only to this world but to me as well.

It hurts to see you choosing bitterness and blame, but **I forgive** you. And **I ask for your forgiveness** too, for not being a perfect mom/dad. **I want to bless us** with an honest relationship: I refuse to be your scapegoat. Your life is your own responsibility and your own choice. Please know that the door of my house and my heart will always be open to you, my dear child, but not to your aggression, accusations, and disrespect"

Stage Three: ANGER Turned Outward

This is the stage where parents begin searching for someone to blame, and there's never a shortage of targets.

There are two main types of angry outbursts at this stage.

The first type of anger outburst directed at people or unfavorable circumstances:

> *"My mother-in-law/my own mother interfered in our family life or helped us too much, and that's why we failed as parents."*

> *"My husband/wife abandoned the family, leaving the kids with trauma that's now exploding in my face."*

> *"My daughter-in-law/son-in-law is turning my child against me."*

> *"That so-called 'therapist' who filled their head with nonsense."*

> *"All that garbage on the internet..."*

Once again, we see the classic cocktail of toxic emotions, a neuro-chemical rush acting as an emotional painkiller. And once again, the "Bruce Almighty syndrome" kicks in, like what prodigal adult children experience when they are judging their parents.

This is a dead end.

The way out? **The Healing Sandwich.**

The second type of anger outburst involves "questioning God."

The core questions echo through the Valley of Sorrow at this stage.

Question Number One: "Why me?"

This may sound odd at first, but it reflects a kind of *personal superiority bias*. If our children are still in the fold, we tend to look at other families with prodigals and think:

> *"That could never happen to me! Their kids rejected them because of their mishandling of their upbringings. I saw how they parented: all that hyper-/hypo-control, discipline that was too strict, the wrong tone, too little time spent… But I'm a good parent. I've done everything right."*

> And then one day, the old saying kicks in: *"There's a black sheep in every family."*

> Suddenly, the reality of a prodigal child is no longer someone else's story and pain, but it is also yours.

> Even *your* child, raised with love and care, can choose "the curse" and blame *you* for their decision.

This is the moment for humility and repentance to those you once judged for their "imperfect parenting."

Question Number Two: "God, where are You in this?

How could You let this happen in my life?"

At this point, I often encourage parents to turn to **Psalm 77**:

> *"I remember my songs in the night… You hold my eyelids open; I am so troubled I cannot speak. I consider the days of old, the years long ago… Will the Lord spurn forever and never again be favorable? Has His steadfast love forever ceased? Are His promises at an end for all time?"*

You start pulling out family photo albums…
Watching old videos, where everyone looked so happy.
You remember those tiny hands, that sweet smile.
You think back to reading bedtime stories, family vacations, going to the movies, that first soccer game you cheered at, that first concert you applauded, the first love you worried about…

And now?

All of that warmth seems like a thing of the past.

Now there's only coldness from your adult child, accusations, hostility, and silence.

"Will the Lord reject me forever? Will He never show His favor again?"

"Has His mercy vanished forever?"

"Has God, in His anger, shut off His compassion?"

Take note of this vital truth:

Crying out to God, even in anger and despair, is *normal, healthy, and healing*. It's far more healing than putting on a fake "spiritual" face and pretending your faith is so strong that you see only silver linings in your grief. God values raw honesty over performative piety.

Question Number Three: "How do I go on from here?"

This is the question that leads to Stage Four. It can be compared to:

a mountain pass- will there be a gentle descent ahead, or another grueling climb?

a crossroads in the desert—will you find an oasis or just another mirage?

Now you face a choice: stay trapped in bitterness and complaint or turn toward the path of **Gratitude, Forgiveness, and Blessing**?

"I will consider all Your works and meditate on all Your mighty deeds. Your ways, God, are holy. You are the God who performs miracles!"

The psalmist made his choice; he chose Life filled with Faith, Hope, and Love.

When someone walking through the Valley of Sorrow makes that same choice, they step into Stage Four.

Stage Four: ADAPTATION TO A NEW REALITY

Accept the situation as it is.

Make plans based on this new reality.

Remember that your **life goes on.**

Start seeing your family dynamics through a different lens, without the "prodigal child" in the center of the picture.

Look around and ask yourself: "Who might need my care, my talents, my gifts, my hard-earned experience?"

A lot of people might need you:

> May be your other children?

> Maybe other parents walking the same road of pain?

> Maybe other prodigal kids who've hit the rock bottom and are desperate for a way out?

And here's one more recommendation, one that I give at every step along the Valley of Sorrow:

Stay away from people who...

- lecture you with philosophy, theology, or passing judgement on your "strange spirituality";

- judge your imperfections or point out your past "mistakes";

- dismiss your pain with empty advice like "Don't cry" or "Crying won't help," or "Just trust God and let go";

- hand out vague clichés like "It's gonna be okay" (what does "okay" even mean?) or specific promises like "your kid will come around soon" (Really? How do they know that?

Stay close to people who...

- are willing to *cry with you*, while truly understanding your grief;

- help you move from one stage to the next, never let you stay stuck in denial, guilt, or blame;

- gently guide you toward accepting the loss while still holding on to the value of life and to *yourself*;

- remind you that **Faith, Hope, and Love** are still with you, and that ***life goes on***, even if the miracle you hoped for hasn't happened yet.

About another brother in the parable

If we go back to the parable of the prodigal son, we will notice another key figure in that story: the **elder brother**.

He was what people call *"the good son."*

The one who supported his father in life and in business.

The one who could be trusted to take over the family business.

The one who was mature and responsible.

This son could have been deeply hurt watching his younger brother treat their father so disrespectfully.

He could have been angry with his brother's behavior and judged his recklessness.

Like his father, he had likely considered his younger brother lost/dead to their family and to any real relationship.

On that remarkable day, as he returned from a hard day's work in the fields, the older son heard music and laughter coming from the house. Something unpleasant stirred in his heart. Instead of rushing home to join the celebration, he stopped. Suspicion and resentment bubbled up. He called over one of the servants and asked sharply, "What's going on? What's the meaning of all this?"

Even his question carried a bitter edge: "How dare my father throw a huge celebration without even consulting me?" The answer was:

"Your brother came back alive and well! Your father cooked the fattened calf to celebrate."

The servant's words only fueled the older brother's anger. He flatly refused to go inside, even when the servant urged him. News of this son's rage reached the father. This was supposed to be a day of pure joy, but now there was a bitter aftertaste. The father's heart ached. "My rock, my steady son, won't join the celebration. Why? Maybe he just doesn't understand the reason for the joy."

So the father rose from the feast and went out.

Still overflowing with joy from his younger son's return, the father hoped the eldest would share his happiness. But instead, he was flooded with questions and accusations:

> *"All these years I've been slaving for you, and I never once disobeyed your orders!"*- this son said. It was not true. He was not a slave, but a son, the heir of the household. *"You are my son,"* the father reminded him gently.

> *"You never gave me a young goat to celebrate with my friends!"* This son said.

Another lie. Everything in the father's house already belonged to him. *"My dear son, you are always with me, and all that I have is yours."* Was the father's quiet, loving response.

And then the venom came spilling out, not just against the father, but against the younger brother too:

> *"This son of yours squandered your wealth on prostitutes, and now you kill the fattened calf for him?!"*

> He said *"this son of yours,"* not "my brother." He drenched his words in scorn and hatred, blaming the father for foolishness and weakness.

And in that moment, his words reveal the state of his heart.

Just like the younger son had once done, the older son had now cut his father out of his heart.

He had mentally stripped his father of the right to make his own decisions, especially decisions rooted in love, forgiveness, and grace. He, too, had become *a prodigal.*

And now fresh pain pierces the father's heart: he realizes he had *two* lost sons. One of them is found, but here stands a grown man, bitter and proud, clinging to imagined wounds and self-righteous anger, rather than embracing truth and what really matters. He yells with the false pretenses: "It would've been better if my brother had stayed lost... or dead!"

But the father responds clearly and without hesitation:

> We **have to** celebrate. This is **right.**

> We **must** rejoice because your brother was dead and is alive again.

He was lost and now he's found."

He is your brother, **not a stranger.**

The father gently gives his older son a chance, a chance to come to his senses, to taste the joy of forgiveness and blessing.

> And that's where the parable ends.

> We don't know what happened next.

> Did the older brother go inside?

> Did he forgive?

Did he celebrate?

We're left without answers.

Sadly, in my practice, I often meet such "good" brothers and sisters hardened, bitter, resentful toward their parents, especially when it comes to inheritance.

They live in constant pursuit of "justice" in dividing up the property they did not pay for.

They feel entitled to control who gets what, as if they know what's fair and best.

And **always**, no matter how the situation unfolds, they come away feeling like *they've been cheated*. It is not a question of *what parents should do to keep all their children happy*. It's a matter of their heart:

- to be content with what they've been given or not

- to choose forgiveness, blessings, and care vs. aggression and resentment.

That was the choice for the older brother in the parable.

I do wish a happy ending with the older brother walking into the feast, wrapping his arms around his younger brother, and joining the celebration; then after the music quiets down, the three men, the father and his two sons, sitting down together to talk through what's next: the future of the family, their shared work, the financial strategies…

Back in the early 2000s, my husband Mikhail and I were leading a series of seminars on the nature of addiction for teens aged fifteen to seventeen at a state-run boarding school. Over time, we formed warm relationships with some kids. They did not see us as professors giving a lecture but treated us mentors. One of them was Igor. He was sixteen back then, already smoking (and not just tobacco).

"I really connected with what you said," he told us after one of our sessions. "Could I call you sometimes? Just to talk?

From that day on, Igor and I talked once a week on phone. After he graduated from high school, he moved to another city and enrolled in a technical college. We eventually lost touch.

Years later, after a seminar in a remote town, a young couple came up to me.

"You don't recognize me, do you?"

"Igor?"

We hugged tightly. Igor introduced his lovely wife:

"This is Raya."

Raya handed me a paper gift bag with an expensive perfume inside.

"This is for you," she said. "Please accept it. It's from all our hearts. You did so much for Igor. And that means you did so much for me, and for our little daughter!"

Igor's eyes glistened with tears.

"You probably don't remember all my friends from boarding school," he said quietly.

"There were six of us. Out of the six, I'm the only one still alive, healthy, happy, and not in prison. It's because, back then, while talking to you, I started making the right choices. I realized that everything in life comes down to a personal choice. Drink or stay sober? I decided. I stayed sober. Sleep around or wait for the right girl? I made a choice. I waited".

This is where Raya leaned into him, smiling, and the dimples on her cheeks lit up.

Igor continued, "Forgive my parents or live in bitterness? I decided. I forgave them.

Every month, since then I send my mom, she lives up north with her new husband, a pizza delivery. It's my reminder to myself: I forgave her. I bless her. And you know what? That's what helps me treasure and love my wife even more, and her parents. They became such amazing grandparents to our daughter and family to me." He gently brushed Raya's hair back.

Whenever I talk to teens, anywhere from twelve to nineteen years old, I always remind them of a few important things:

- **Family** is the very first social group, the circle where you learn to love, to forgive, to care, to admit your mistakes and to grow. It is sad but some teens prefer not to learn any of that and choose to stay stuck in blame and resentment.

- Think of your **family**, the one you're in right now, as a *training camp* for building your future relationships. It's where you develop the core skills of being human and learning how to connect.

- Once you step out of childhood (around age ten or eleven), the saying *"your life is in your hands"* becomes real, and it doesn't glitch. Whatever you personally choose, **how you treat yourself and those close to you will shape all your future relationships**.

When you were born, your mom and dad were fully responsible for the parent–child relationship. As you grow older, you gradually start to participate in it too and in your teens the responsibility begins shifting: **the quality of relationship depends on what *you* choose to do**.

Your parents gave you what they could do. They raised you the best they knew how. They taught you what they knew.

Until you turn eighteen, being legally responsible for keeping you clothed, fed, safe, and educated, they offered and showed you, their values. But when it comes to shaping **your personal values and worldview**, that's *your* choice now, when you turn twelve.

Most psychologists stress the importance of personality development during the teenage years and consider it essential for building resilience against risky, destructive, or antisocial behavior. For example, **D. Elkonin** identifies two kinds of the teen's readiness for becoming an adult:

- **objective readiness** refers to outward signs of maturity: work, study, peer relationships, personal appearance, responsible romantic relationships, etc.

- **subjective readiness** is the inner, social, and moral component; it shows up as the ability to stand by one's own opinions, defend personal views and moral values, and engage in self-education.

So, if a teenager just "goes with the crowd" without their own views, drowning in bitter emotions, ignoring their responsibilities and blaming parents and/or the whole world, that teen is choosing *not* to grow up.

According to **D. Feldstein**, signs of growing up described by Elkonin only matter if the teenager is trying to express themselves creatively through meaningful work and relationships. But if a teen tries to prove themselves by holding grudges and making demands, tearing down relationships because of selfish ambitions, blaming others (including God) then they are consciously refusing to grow up. This attitude is dangerous, both for themselves and for everyone around them.

G. Collins says that adolescence is primarily the time to choose your own identity, when a teen tries to answer key questions that define who they are:

"Who am I?" (personal identity):

Who am I as a son/a daughter? As a brother/a sister? As a man /a woman? As a future professional: doctor, businessperson, builder? As a future family member: husband/wife, father/mother?

"What am I like? What do I believe in?" (moral values and beliefs determine the kind of personality):

Do I believe in the family values or I'm on my own? Do I believe in love, or just sex? Do I believe in the power of relationships, or in the power of money? Do I believe in commitment, or in using people? Do I believe it's important to care for my parents, or am I only responsible for my own kids?

"Who am I with?" (social identity and status):

Am I with people who value morals and ethics, or with those who promote egoism and pleasure? Am I with people who care about family values, or those who preach freedom from any responsibility? Am I around honest people with strong integrity, or with those who live recklessly?

V.V. Ryzhov points out how today's media, the internet and pop culture bombard young people with conflicting and often unrealistic images of "how life should be." Many get lost in the noise and end up in the danger zone. Others stay stuck in an endless search for something to anchor their sense of self.

To me, it's clear: people end up in a danger zone when they get hooked on all the buzzwords about "personal boundaries," "total separation," "self-assertion by any means," "childhood wounds" and "parents-to-blame".

THE QUALITY OF YOUR LIFE
IS IN YOUR HANDS

It all depends on the choices you make: whom to listen to, whom to follow, what to believe in. Those who decide to wear the mask of victims of childhood trauma, who dive deep into blaming others, who ignore values like love, loyalty, commitment, and responsibility, and who gather around them like-minded people to justify the mess in their life - are choosing to remain immature.

Elkonin describes four main patterns of **maladaptive identity development**:

- **Withdrawal from close relationships**. It means turning real feelings into something fake or just shutting yourself off. So don't listen to popular stuff from pseudo specialists like: "It's totally normal for a teen to ignore their parents and family events." Do not support the behavior of *maladaptive identity development*

- **Temporal disorientation**, where the person avoids making plans due to anxiety and fear of change. Then stop digging endlessly in your childhood traumas according to the trendy strategy; it keeps you stagnant: bitterness, blame, and aggression anchor you in the past, locking into a cycle of "processing" instead of progressing. It is a part of *maladaptive identity development*

- **Loss of capacity for productive work**, marked by poor focus, avoidance of external engagement, and inability to tap into their own resources. How could a "chronically in-resentment" young adult yelling, "I didn't ask you to have me!" possibly engage in meaningful activity? No way. But they are kept in this condition by modern trend: "Parents had kids for their own pleasure, so children owe them nothing, not to their parents, not to society. Everyone owes them, but they owe no one." Stop listening to all that nonsense! It feeds *maladaptive identity development.*

- **Negative identity**, where the person rejects or even despises roles which would be considered normative in their family or culture. This may include rejecting their name, gender, cultural identity, values, feeling-orientation.

  Mantras like:

  "Only do what feels good."

  "Cut ties with anyone who doesn't serve and/or support you."

  "Life's too short to waste on other people's needs."

  These are seductive but shallow slogans rooted in hedonism which is a foundation for *maladaptive identity development.*

The typical portrait of *an adult with maladaptive identity:*

- Bitter at the world

- Perpetually blaming others in everything

- Restless with their own failures

- Obsession with blaming their parents

- Lack of responsibility for their own lives.

They all say that it's unfair to "let parents off the hook," and tell shocking stories of abuse.

I am not ignorant. I know that there are parents who are alcoholics, criminals, and those who abandon their babies in hospitals. But they're a small percentage of all families.

Frankly speaking I have never met a mom or a dad who said: "My dream is to make my child's life miserable and turn him into an aggressive individual or an alcoholic."

On the other hand, the number of angry grown-up kids, blaming their "toxic" parents, is much higher and growing faster.

I always ask this key question at my meetings and seminars with parents: "Who's really responsible for the quality of parent-child relationships, the parents or the child?"

About 90% say "the parents."

A few say, "both sides."

Neither of these two answers is completely right. The answer depends on the child's age.

To support my point of view, I'll refer to the classic theories of human development by the great psychologists **Erik Erikson, Jean Piaget,** and **Lawrence Kohlberg**.

First, I would like to present their findings on the

Early Childhood Development (Before Adolescence)

Erik Erikson, with his theory of psychosocial development, divided the pre-adolescent years into four stages:

- **Infancy (0–1 year-olds)**: their foundation of trust in the world is either laid or broken; through consistent nurturing and stable **relationships especially with the mother** the child learns to feel secure in having their basic needs met; ideally, the child can endure her temporary absence without distress, being confident she will return.

- **Early Childhood (1–3-year-olds)**: at this stage, other family members, especially the father, enter the relational world of the child who starts learning autonomy, overcoming shame and doubt; **both parents** must align expectations with the child's developmental stage, balancing discipline and freedom so that the emerging "I can do it myself" attitude outweighs impulsivity or blind compliance.

- **Preschool (3–6-year-olds)**: The child's **immediate environment** either nurtures initiative or suppresses it; with adult guidance (parents, grandparents, other members of the family), moral responsibility for actions begins to form. Clear boundaries ("what is allowed / what is not") are essential, but overloading the child's conscience with guilt or fear can stifle initiative, leading to a fragile, fear-driven personality.

- **School Age (6–12 years)**: the focus shifts to developing diligence, learning new skills, and building a sense of competence; without adult support, feelings of inferiority and inadequacy can take root, leading to poor peer relationships and low self-esteem.

  Key point: Erikson underscores the crucial role of parents, not just in nurturing but in instilling social norms and behavioral expectations.

Jean Piaget studied cognitive development; he identified the following pre-adolescent stages:

- **Sensorimotor Stage (0–2 years)**: intellectual growth happens through coordination of sensory experiences (like mom's smile or dad's playful noises) with physical actions (like dropping toys repeatedly and deliberately to see what happens).

- **Preoperational Stage (2–7 years)**: children begin forming mental representations relying on intuition rather than logic (e.g., "the wind blows because the trees are moving").

- **Concrete Operational Stage (7–11 years)**: being capable of logical reasoning about concrete situations, children can draw conclusions and understand cause and effect but still need tangible examples and adult guidance.

   Key point: Piaget saw adult involvement as critical for steering intellectual growth. He didn't support the idea of trendy modern specialists that "children develop best when left entirely with their interests and desires".

Lawrence Kohlberg, in his theory of moral development, spoke about two levels before adolescence:

- **Preconventional Morality**: the child obeys rules to avoid punishment or gain rewards and acts with self-centered motivation.

- **Conventional Morality**: children start following rules not just for self-interest but to maintain good relationships and gain approval from authority figures.

   Key point: A structured system of rewards, consequences, respect for authority, and desire for approval are vital for moral development. The popular philosophy of "child-centered families," where everything revolves around the child's whims and against discipline - works against this process.

The Shift in Responsibility happens in Adolescence

Erik Erikson writes that from ages 12 to 19, individuals **form their identity**. Here, they reflect on their character, social roles, and aspirations. They begin to evaluate their strengths and weaknesses, aiming to improve themselves. As the adolescent makes choices independently, the process of forming identity cannot be left unattended.

Jean Piaget observed that from age 11, cognitive development enters the **formal operational stage**, where adolescents can think abstractly and hypothetically. Now, they choose what to do with the knowledge and moral lessons imparted to them. Teens begin to make independent decisions about how to use the knowledge, information, and judgments they have received. They need the judgment as a measure for their decisions.

Lawrence Kohlberg noted that from 11 or 12 onward, individuals begin developing **autonomous morality**, an internalized sense of right and wrong guided by conscience. First, they focus on the well-being of those around them and fulfilling commitments. Later, they may embrace universal ethical principles that guide behavior beyond social approval. Teens need supportive adults who can help strengthen their moral convictions.

Parents should remember: your responsibility is to keep the teens' life in order, but above all your main responsibility is to instill values into your growing child. When our children are teens, the following dogma is essential: **you can and you must teach**

your children to say "thank you" but you cannot make their hearts grateful.

In other words, remember the proverbs which have equivalents in all languages:

- *No garden is without its weeds.*

- *There is a black sheep in every flock.*

- *Many a good cow has an evil calf.*

All of these are about the same reality: even in healthy, loving families, someone may choose a destructive path.

It's simply not fair to insist that:

"Parents always reap what they've sown."

"If a child is disrespectful, it's because the parents modeled that behavior."

"If a teenager starts stealing or using drugs, it's entirely the parents' fault."

"If a parent can't maintain a good relationship with their adolescent child, it's 100% their responsibility."

This endless list of "quotes" from popular specialists has nothing to do with classical psychology. From adolescence onward, every person is fully responsible for their own choices.

And isn't it ironic how the very same "guru influencers" who put all the blame on parents also preach about *"freedom of choice"*, *"personal responsibility to challenge toxic patterns"*, and *"the power of self-determination"*.

I can't help but ask them:

How do these high-sounding principles fit with the fatalistic mantra "you're a product of your parents"?

Is there a free will of a person to be the "black sheep," or not?

In Conclusion

There are two equally important messages in this longest chapter of the book: one for parents and one for adult children.

PARENTS, avoid falling into extremes, don't spend your life consumed by grief over your prodigal children, and don't let yourself harden into lifelong bitterness toward them either. The healthy, balanced response is the one we see in the father from the parable of the prodigal son.

ADULT CHILDREN, the quality of your life is in your own hands. It does not depend on what your parents gave you (or didn't give), but on what you choose to do with all of that. What will you cultivate: wheat (blessings, forgiveness, gratefulness, care) or weeds (resentment, aggression, bitterness, separation)?

Wishing all of us wisdom and love.

CHAPTER FIVE

TRAUMATIC AND PSEUDO-TRAUMATIC FAMILIES

Widespread expressions of outrage have accused me of downplaying the concept of "childhood trauma."

In classical psychology, this term is closely connected with PTSD, post-traumatic stress disorder which can be triggered by events such as:

- a threat to life (not only your own, but also that of those you hold dear), whether real or perceived;

- sexual abuse, acts of physical violence or severe cruelty, whether directly endured or observed, including those inflicted upon animals;

- witnessing the death of another individual or an animal;

- exposure to war or armed conflict, especially as a prolonged situation of danger and instability;

- being diagnosed with a life-threatening disease, getting permanently disabled, or experiencing an overwhelming sense of helplessness in the face of irreversible change;

- natural disasters, terrorist attacks, industrial accidents, or other catastrophes that evoke a deep sense of vulnerability and loss of control.

In real-life cases of PTSD, therapy - often long-term (not a lifelong), is essential in helping a person process the trauma, grieve what was lost, and gradually reclaim a sense of purpose and vitality.

Ultimately, effective therapy for PTSD is not about endlessly dissecting 'toxic parents' or obsessively searching for a scapegoat.

Let me share a true story.

Two young sisters, both were sexually abused by their older half-brother. He was their father's son from a previous marriage. The boy was fifteen, when he began molesting the older sister, who was only thirteen at the time. Later, he began taking advantage of the younger one, starting when she was only eleven. He used classic exploitative tactics to manipulate and control the girls, slowly wearing down their self-esteem by poisoning them with lies like:

"You deserve this treatment."
"You should feel unbelievably lucky to please me."
"You're worthless."

And sad, the girls started to believe him.

The story of the older sister, Vera.

At 16, she went to a youth camp where she heard something that struck a chord:

"You are worthy. You are beautiful. God loves you. He has an incredible plan for your life. You are a precious jewel."

Something inside her shifted. She cried for hours, not knowing why she felt both joy and deep sorrow, unsettling yet freeing all at once. For several days she would sneak away alone into the woods, lie face down in the soft grass, and weep. Eventually, she confided in a spiritual councilor that she had been sexually abused for 3 years. With her permission, he contacted her parents, urging them to attend a discussion about the incident. (At that time, there was no requirement to disclose such cases to authorities; disclosure occurred only when the victim chose to do so).

When her parents heard what happened to Vera, they were horrified, but not at the abuser and his actions. Instead, they were upset that their daughter had compromised "the family name." They insisted:

"It couldn't have been that bad. Vera must have provoked this boy somehow."

For Vera, this was a severe blow. She declined the councilor's offer to "untangle the whole mess," saying she would not press charges, and if he did, she would deny everything. Still, she accepted his help: she withdrew from school, enrolled in a Christian college, and moved into student housing.

It wasn't until six months later, when her half-brother was arrested for armed robbery and was put in jail that her parents finally accepted the facts of his wrongdoing. Nevertheless, they continued to "protect" him and posted bail for his release. Within a week, while under house arrest, he was killed in a gang-related dispute in their backyard.

Over time, Vera's mother began visiting her more often at college. One day, her father called and said:

"Sweetheart, it's safe for you to come home now. I'm so sorry that our home used to be a dangerous place for you."

Vera came home. They cried together. They forgave each other. Their bond was restored.

By the time her mother shared this story with me, Vera was already married and expecting her first child.

Her mother sought my help with her younger daughter Tatiana, who was 21 at the time. Following the death of her abuser, Tatiana was in a deep depression for over five years. Medication provided only fleeting relief. Her mother said: "Tatiana's depression is like a black hole getting deeper every day. She swings from extreme insomnia to sleeping for days. She is either irritable beyond reason or lost in a fog, disconnected from time and space. She picks her skin and rips her hair out in distress. She has a lot of hatred towards her sister Vera, and me."

I was gentle but told her firmly: I do not give consultations through a third party. Your twenty-one-year-old daughter lives her own life.

"But she will never come to see you! She calls psychologists 'head-fixers.' She is very skeptical of people, and she never talks about the past."

I suggested she let Tatiana know about a seminar I was hosting soon for young adults (ages 16–25) on Building Personal Resilience. I handed her an invitation: "Tell your daughter that this ticket isn't for a 'scary mind-fixer' or a 'dangerous brainwashing session,' but for a warm gathering in a cozy room with a nice group of people. Besides the seminar, there will be time for chatting over tea and an opportunity to engage in interactive youth activities. And if she feels comfortable there, and can resonate with what I am going to share, then it will be easier for her to seek help..."

Tatiana's story as she told me:

Tatiana was 14 when her parents came home from visiting Vera at camp. At home, they asked a lot of questions, but it was clear they were not on Vera's side. Tatiana realized that her parents were deeply disappointed and upset with Vera for telling an outsider about what happened to her. She took her parents' side and said, "It is not as bad as Vera made it sound." Tatiana's parents appeared relieved. Late that night, when her brother came home, they confronted him with the truth of what had transpired. At first, he was frightened, but he regained his composure once he realized he wasn't in any real danger. Vera backed off, the parents chose not to intervene, and Tatiana stood by him. He even made a few jokes about Vera: «Silly little drama queen was always good at making up the stories." Something in Tatiana changed. She felt a rush of hatred toward her older sister mixed with an unexpected burst of joy: "I don't have to share him with my sister anymore."

Though, Tatiana was unfamiliar with the term 'Stockholm syndrome", yet her reality embodied it. She saw the monster who abused and humiliated her as a desired man in her life.

She cried when he was sentenced to go to jail, insisted on private visits with him, and surprised the guards with her persistence and raising their suspicions. They contacted her parents and shared their concerns. As a result, her parents did not allow her to visit him in prison anymore. This led to intense arguments and a lot of drama at home. Tatiana went through an emotional rollercoaster when her brother was discharged from the house arrest. She was terrified that "the sexual encounter would happen again" mixed with hope that "maybe this time it will be more pleasant". Every time "after it happened," she would go to the shower and vigorously scrub herself with a loofah, swallowing tears, sometimes vomiting because of disgust of what she had endured during the latest experience. It was the other side of her life: part of her had always been aware of the horror this man brought into her life and all the damage he caused. After his death, she fell into deep despair.

When Vera was going to get married two years after her brother's murder, Tatiana got very angry with her sister:

"How dare she forget everything?!" She texted Vera's fiancé many horrible details of their past. But Vera's fiancé knew about Vera's pain: he was among the few who were let in on the secret at the youth camp. They went to the same college together. Watching Vera every day, he was amazed by her inner beauty and purity of someone who had been through so much. He and Vera understood the deep meaning of Tatiana's messages: she was hurting. Yet, Tatiana overwhelmed by her anger and resentment was unable to break free from their grip. She refused to believe it was possible to wash away her dirty past. She saw her sister Vera as a hypocrite.

Tatiana also hated her mother vengeance: "How could she let all this happen?!" By "all this," she meant the abuse, the ban on visiting their brother in prison, and the fact that she "didn't save him..."

Towards their father, Tatiana felt complete silence: "He was responsible for bringing a worthless son into this world!"

She was upset how well Vera and her parents got along: "Hypocrites!"

Years of hatred, resentment, shame, and guilt; these poisonous emotions turned her life into hell.

...Tatiana was stunned when I started talking about forgiveness.

"Are you serious?! My therapist is sounding like a broken record when he tells me to "let go of the past, let go of the past', that's ridiculously funny. But you are even more ridiculous now with your forgiveness."

It took time for her to understand some simple truths in close connection to each other:

- you can't "let go" of the past if you haven't forgiven,

- forgiveness is impossible if you haven't voiced your pain,

- there's no point in voicing your pain if you find satisfaction in nursing your sufferings,

- clinging to pain is a choice that delays your readiness to mature,

- you won't mature until you fully go through the Valley of Sorrow.

Her healing began when she said aloud: "I forgive the monster..."

The words "monster" and "forgive" were like a mountain she couldn't climb. It was her own Mountain Everest.

She was stunned to realize how her "humiliated self" clung to the warped patterns of loyalty and yearning for her abusive brother. His lies were stuck in her brain, *"He's the only one you deserve. He's yours, and you are his."*

Identifying him for what he truly was, a man who violated her, was the first step towards healing. Speaking those words out loud was the beginning of "voicing her pain." And then came the next impossible step: *"I forgive..."*

This was the beginning of her journey out of the Valley of Sorrow, where she stayed for years. Later she created many Healing

Sandwiches for her Mom, Dad, and her sister. Several weeks later her doctor changed her medication, because she didn't need the strong ones anymore.

Growing Up: Sign of Mature Personality

A grown, mature person can make choices which are aligned with their true self and with their place in a bigger world.

Let's compare the signs of maturity with the traits of those who cling to immature way of thinking:

Emotional stability vs. heightened emotionality

Tatiana followed the recommendations for restoring emotional balance and preventing depression through natural methods as physical activity, balanced nutrition, reading, limited screen time, connecting with people of faith, conversations with mentors...

Flexibility vs. rigid black-and-white thinking

When Tatiana accepted her parents' imperfections and let go of her rigid divisions of the world into "good" and "evil," she found new flexibility in her relationships with family members.

Healthy caution vs. recklessness

Her fear that "I'll never be able to have a normal relationship with a man because I loved an abuser" shifted to "My past is like a preventive vaccination: I can now clearly distinguish between a safe relationship and a dangerous one."

Ability to process past experiences vs. rejecting the past

Her earlier stance of "I don't want to talk about it" and "I just want to forget it like a bad dream" turned into the process of "turning crap into fertilizer."

Connecting the present to a vision of the future vs. "nurturing the past and living without perspective

Tatiana became involved in a volunteer initiative focused on HIV/AIDS prevention, working specifically with teenage girls at a boarding school. She realized she enjoyed mentoring girls at crossroads in their lives. One day, a thought came to her mind: "What if I became a teacher?" At first, she dismissed it, but later she began preparing to apply for a distance-learning program in education.

Standing firm in one's beliefs vs. dissolving into others' opinions

Over time, Tatiana became one of the leaders in the project for teenage girls, guiding others with conviction and compassion.

This transformation revealed a key truth to Tatiana:

The process of maturity depends less on external factors (environment and circumstances) and more on internal ones (personal decisions). This is the principal she adopted alongside the Healing Sandwich method and an aphorism of my husband's, which became her favorite:

"We can take our life's crap and turn it into fertilizer.

Anyone taking this principle to heart stops the process of multiplying the life's crap but enjoys the life flourishing everywhere because of having fertilizer. It also occurs with PTSD and in the process of eliminating abuse in families.

To avoid confusion, I want to pause and take a closer look at the term "abuse" —particularly because I disagree with one of its most widely accepted definitions today:

> ☹ **"Abuse is any interaction intended to assert or preserve control over another individual through the use of force."**

In my humble opinion, this definition does not reflect the reality of what people typically mean when they talk about abuse. Taken literally, this definition suggests that every person on earth commits the acts of abuse and/or gets abused daily—solely due to the inherent structure of human society.

- Most of us are forced to wake up at a certain time to go to work or school because someone sets a schedule for us. Furthermore, the individual who determines the schedule holds the power to enforce it through punitive measures—such as withholding pay, reducing bonuses, imposing fines, or terminating employment. Would this be defined as abuse?

- We "abuse" our children by not letting them play video games all night, not allowing them to eat junk food and drink soda all day, stopping them from running around naked in the house or outside. Doesn't it seem like children are subjected to countless forms of 'abuse' in their everyday life?

- By this definition, we are 'abusing' our neighbors when we enforce public smoking bans or object to them turning their front lawn into a dumping ground. We call the authorities, confront the neighbors, and use various legal options to make them follow the laws. Is it appropriate to consider us abusers?

By this logic, all laws and social norms are various forms of "abuse."

Don't steal! - But what if I feel like it?

Don't kill! - But what if someone really makes me angry?

Do not commit assault! - But what if I want to punish someone?

You are subjecting me to "abuse" if you deny me the freedom to do what I want when I am not allowed to.

I am being deliberately sarcastic here, because while the popular definition is absurd on its one hand, on the other hand it is often weaponized and used as a starting point to distort the meaning of 'abuse' by getting people wrapped up in toxic emotions like shame, fear, guilt, and resentment.

I personally prefer the term **"deliberate cruel treatment"** as a synonym to "abuse". It is a more concrete and precise definition. **Abuse as cruel treatment is any deliberate actions or inactions that cause harm to physical, mental, or spiritual health of an individual or a living thing.**

It is true, that experiencing or witnessing domestic physical abuse within the household is very traumatic for the child. But what do you personally mean when you say, "physical abuse"? Sadly, in today's contemporary society, any physical discipline by a parent is frequently categorized as 'beating' or 'abuse. But consider a ballet teacher at a ballet school: instead of endlessly repeating "keep your back straight," they might give a light tap on the shoulder blades. No one calls this "abuse" because there is no deliberate action to harm.

Grabbing children firmly by the hand when they rush onto a busy street; carrying them out of a store where they are throwing a tantrum on the floor; pulling them out of a fight they started with another child; these are all physical actions. Would we consider them cruel deliberate attempts to hurt a child? No. They are not any deliberate actions to harm. Yet, many specialists, when unpacking "childhood trauma," convince their clients that such "abuse" deeply scars the "fragile soul" of a child and is the "root of the child's future struggles". It is nonsense. Child's neurotic system is flexible and restores quickly especially if the system of discipline is logical, predictable and accompanied with care and love.

To some extent I understand educators and psychologists who oppose *any* physical discipline; in most cases, they base their views on the severe cases when parents deliberately harm their child. However, such parents are very rare. But the industry of "childhood traumas" based on "abuse-everywhere-syndrome" is flourishing, ruining family systems and child development.

Witnessing abuse toward either parent is also traumatic for a child. Spousal relationships are in the heart of every family. Children are highly sensitive to discord, unresolved conflicts, abuse, and breakdowns between their parents. On the other hand, it is not always about yelling or breaking dishes. Sometimes abuse hides under a facade of a quiet presence.

There are families where conflicts are loud and fiery, but it is not always abuse. They may be as I call them "loud italian families" with two expressive personalities hashing things out. For children, it is a communication style. Please understand that I do not agree with this style, but it is not necessarily an abuse. True abuse is marked by fear followed by shame and guilt: a mother who walks on eggshells, afraid to anger or upset her husband; an abusive individual dominates every disagreement not as a loving head of the household but as a tyrant.

Nevertheless, even if you went through real abuse in your family as a child, your adult life is not a product of your past but your choice to see it as drama or as fertilizer. As I mentioned before, up to about the age of 10, children are shaped by their environment and especially their parents. An abusive home is undeniably harmful. But when grown men and women point fingers decades later, saying, "I can't be happy and/or behave myself because of my parents' toxic marriage" it sounds strange.

…A woman once told me about her husband:

"He is aggressive and curses a lot, even hits me. But deep down, he is a good man. He is traumatized because his mother was so harsh on him."

"Really?" I replied, "And why was his mother so harsh?"

"Yes, yes!" the woman eagerly jumps on the childhood trauma bandwagon. "My mother-in-law said her dad was too demanding, never gave anyone a break."

"Oh wow, that's interesting! And what trauma did your mother-in-law's dad have?"

"His mom was a tough woman after the war, she raised the kids alone, no time for tenderness…"

"Are you hearing yourself?" I intervened before she began projecting her husband's difficulties onto a relative, assigning misplaced blame. "Your husband, a forty-year-old man, behaves terribly, and you are blaming his great-great-grandmother! At this rate, we will reach Adam and Eve soon enough while your husband remains pure and innocent. No, that's not how it works—he alone is responsible for choosing to engage in harmful behavior."

The woman was shocked-it was a new perspective that shattered her long-held beliefs about blaming her great-grandparents for the life's difficulties.

In adulthood, the concept of "a happy childhood" directly relates to the individual's current state of wellbeing. As a rule, accomplished adults who built their own families maintain warm relationships with their parents and ancestors. They succeed professionally, and they tend to remember their childhood in a positive light. They perceive their parents' past "flaws" with humor, warmth, and gratitude for the good things. They realize that their parents are imperfect but loving. Those who choose gratitude, forgiveness, and blessing reap great rewards: their memories of childhood are full of joy.

On the other hand, there are others who live with demanding attitudes toward life, with unshakable belief that their parents owe them endlessly. By choosing resentment and hatred, these individuals determine the outcomes of their own actions: childhood memories become steeped in misery and bitterness, framed by the belief that they were mistreated and insufficiently loved

In many families, siblings fall on different ends of the spectrum, experiencing life in distinct ways. Much of this depends on how they choose to interpret their experiences.

Viktor Frankl, the psychiatrist and founder of logotherapy, one of the most influential representative of existential schools of psychotherapy, believed that the root of all psychological problems lies in a sense of meaninglessness, when a person fails to find purpose in life. He taught that the pursuit of meaning is the antidote to this emptiness. According to Frankl, chasing pleasure without having meaning of life leads only to frustration. A life driven solely by personal desires often obstructs the pursuit of deeper meaning and can spiral into neurosis.

When life feels devoid of meaning, peace and joy slip away. People drift in an existential vacuum—until they discover their unique purpose. Frankle was sure that no specialist can provide that meaning for the client, but they can guide a person toward it. Frankl also emphasized personal responsibility, asserting that everyone is accountable for their choices and actions.

Based on his research and observations, Frankl identified certain values that give life its meaning:

- **Creative values** – what we give to the world, to others, and to humanity.

- **Experiential values** – what we receive from the world, from relationships, from life itself.

- **Attitudinal values** – how we choose to respond to situations we cannot change.

What does this mean in practice? The life of each person carries meaning and worth. Even individuals with physical or mental disabilities may not engage in creative or experiential values—but they can still embody attitudinal values. They are still someone's son, daughter, sibling, spouse, or friend. Their life is interwoven into the value systems of the people around them.

Frankl also argued that freedom isn't about *"freedom from"* something but it's about *"freedom for"* embracing responsibility.

And yet, it is the pursuit of "freedom from" that drives those who remain entangled in past wounds—nurturing bitterness, fear, shame, and guilt. True healing begins with forgiveness, gratitude, and the act of blessing; each a vital expression of agape of love. This love, unconditional and selfless, must extend to oneself, to others, and to God, regardless of how unjust or painful one's circumstances may have been.

Once a woman came to me for counseling overwhelmed with guilt toward her children. For the past five years, her family had been a refuge for those passing away: first for her husband's grandmother, dying of cancer, who was dearly loved by the whole family; then for her father, who never fully recovered after a stroke and needed constant care until his death from a heart attack; and then her mother, who broke her hip and now the entire family—including her husband and their teenage children—provided care for the grandmother.

"I understand my kids could be going out and hanging out more with their friends," the woman broke down, "but they have to help with the caregiving."

"Have to?" I asked. "Do they do it grudgingly, after arguments and complaints?"

"No! They understand that these are our cherished family members!"

"Honey, right now your children are going through the best life experience possible. And what does your husband say about all of this?"

"You won't believe it, but he says the same thing you do, that everything has its own time, and its own value and that this is the best time to love our family members who don't' have much time left on this earth."

It is crucial for the people, especially teenagers, to understand this simple truth: **think of your family as a gym for the soul—a place where you train in the essential virtues of life. It's where you practice caring and forgiveness, learn to admit mistakes and ask for forgiveness, and grow in the art of accepting others**

with their flaws. As a result, you live a fulfilling life loving and being loved.

But if you see your family as a prison, a system that suppresses your individuality, as an oppressive force of control—then you're headed for a dead end where growth and fulfillment become impossible.

According to leading existential psychologists and counselors, alienation from higher values is a primary cause of life's meaninglessness and psychological emptiness.

Søren Kierkegaard, father of existentialism, identified five core elements of human existence: conscience, love, fear, care, and determination. Kierkegaard believed that the root of all emotional and spiritual struggles lay in an existential crisis—the alienation from God and His values. A devoted admirer of Hegel, he borrowed the concept that Hegel called *"the failure to perceive the transcendent (the Divine)."* In his pastoral work, Kierkegaard made it his primary focus to awaken in people the capacity to perceive the Divine, which includes embracing moral standards, taking responsibility for one's life, and caring for others.

Karl Jaspers—a philosopher, psychologist, and psychiatrist, said that all emotional and psychological disorders stem from three destructive principles of human existence:

- Rationality elevated to an absolute, where the surrounding world is seen empirically, as a substance to be classified and calculated; this kind of rationality diminishes the importance of love, forgiveness, and gratitude because they cannot be measured, calculated, or empirically studied, and therefore there could be a risk of them being ignored by those who prioritize reason above all.

- Self-centeredness and the objectification of others manifest when an individual becomes the center of the universe and everything around them, including relationships with family, is evaluated through the lens of personal gain: *"Is this useful or not? Should I maintain this relationship, or it ran its course and it's time to end it?"*

- Self-assertion through the stance " I can do myself", coupled with the rejection of God and universal moral principles, leads to a perception of morality as ambiguous, and subject to negotiation.

Jaspers argued that people either embrace these destructive principles and descend into moral bankruptcy or reject them and experience transformation by discovering unconditional virtuous principles like care, forgiveness, and love.

Boris Bratus, a psychologist and scholar who pioneered research on personality and the behavior regulation, believed that the quality of human life depends directly on the depth of meaning one cultivates:

- **Egocentric level** – where a person is focused solely on their own desires, preferences, emotions, and decisions, guided only by self-interest.

- **Group-centric level** – where one's sense of value and life choices begin to consider the needs and interests of their group (e.g., family).

- **Humanistic level** – where all people are valued equally, regardless of group affiliation, and choices are based on moral principles.

- **Moral consciousness level** – where a person understands their life and their responsibility within the vast history of humanity and its existence.

- **Eschatological level** – where one recognizes their accountability to the Creator for how they live and how they realize their potential.

The role of a psychologist, according to Bratus, is to help people move beyond the egocentric level and to overcome their narrow focus on personal needs to develop a broader vision of existence and growth.

In Conclusion

Every painful experience in your life can either become a life-long trap, or it can be transformed into a profound blessing by giving you an ability to empathize, understand, accept, and serve those around you.

Parenting is about imparting values, not merely feeding and raising a child.

However, parents are not gods. I will say it again: you can teach your child to say, "thank you", and you should. What you cannot do is place a grateful heart inside their chest. That part is up to them.

CHAPTER SIX

THE COST OF CARRYING RESENTMENT

Many years ago, when Mikhail and I were about to get married, we were both students. I was in my second year at the teacher's college, and my fiancé was in his fifth year at the aviation university. Mikhail worked part-time as a freelance photographer, and I worked early mornings cleaning offices in a large institution. We decided to have a modest wedding, paid for with our own small savings, so we carefully trimmed down the guest list. At that time, both my parents and Mikhail's parents were divorced. For me, there was no question whether to invite my dad to the wedding. Obviously, I was going to invite him! Even though he had left my mom for another woman two years earlier, he returned a decade later. Looking back, I witnessed how their relationship grew warm and close again—proof of the healing power of forgiveness and my mother's remarkable grace. He fully enjoyed the blessing of the restored family connection: spending time with us, his daughters, and grandchildren. Yet, while we were planning the wedding, my dad lived with another woman. I invited my dad anyway, and he accepted my condition to attend my wedding without his girlfriend. For me, it was natural because he was still my father and a dear person in my life regardless of all the pain his betrayal caused our family.

What really surprised me was that my fiancé decided not to invite his father. I knew the story of his childhood and his relationship with his dad. All his memories were the scenes of his father coming home drunk, yelling and hitting his mother, while little Mikhail, four or five years old, ran around trying to "shoot" his father with a toy gun. In the eyes of the child, the drunkard was a monster in his dad's body. One day when Mikhail's dad brought home a drunk and rude woman, little Mikhail had to "shoot" two monsters from his toy gun, while his older brother, then fourteen, stood up to protect their mother. That day, the father kicked the mother and his two sons out of their house. For three years, they wandered from relatives to friends, lived in the hostels, until his mom was granted a small room in a communal apartment. Throughout these years, their father never offered any help. I deeply understood my husband's decision not to invite that man to our wedding.

About ten years have passed. So much transpired during that time. We left our hometown Samara for the Russian Far East, where my husband served as an officer; then we returned to our hometown. We dealt with our housing issues by moving from one apartment to another; we overcame a family crisis, found our footing and came to faith in God.

One Saturday, there was a knock on the door. I went to open the door and found a middle-aged man there whom I could not recognize. He looked me straight in the eyes and asked:

"Are you Nadezhda?"

I nodded, racking my brain to place him.

"Is Mikhail home?" He asked next, and chills ran down my spine.

It was as if my eyes opened wide, and right before me stood my husband: same posture, same height, same eyes, same hair, only now it was gray.

I got chills all over my body. What is going to happen now?

Unconsciously, I stepped aside, and the man walked past me into the hallway.

From the room, my husband called out:

"Nadya, who's there?"

I couldn't answer; my mouth froze. Mikhail walked in the hallway and stopped. I can still picture it clearly: father and son standing face to face. Only a meter between them and it felt like a lifetime.

Time crawled as his father said:

"Son, forgive me for all the pain I caused you. As a gesture of peace, I offer you this sack of dried, salty fish—caught from the Volga River and dried with care, just for you. I know how much you love it.

He handed Mikhail a paper bag filled with dried fish (Russian delicacy).

A few more seconds of eternity passed, then my husband stepped forward and hugged his father.

That day, I fell in love with my husband all over again. It's a rare and priceless gift to live with someone who knows how to forgive. Later, as we sat in the kitchen sipping tea with his father, Mikhail shared that in recent weeks, he'd felt an urge in his heart to find his dad, make peace, and ask forgiveness for not inviting him to our wedding.

Two years later, his father died of a heart attack. Those two years became a season of deep friendship between our family and him, bringing warmth and shared affection into our lives. We never pretended those "missing years" were not there. Mikhail's father was still married to another woman, and when he passed away, my husband didn't pursue any inheritance rights. It was no longer about property or obligation, but it was about two men choosing relationship despite the twenty years they had no contact with each other. As a result, our daughters had two grandfathers! And the lesson learned is to cherish your family.

When I share this story, people often say: "But your father-in-law came first and asked to forgive him. That's why there was a happy ending." But forgiveness isn't about <u>who</u> makes the first move. It's about the state of your heart. If your heart is full of bitterness and resentment, even the sincerest attempts at reconciliation will seem:

"Not genuine enough."

"Driven by selfish motives."

"Forced or insincere."

My husband forgave his father long before this man ever came to our door. That forgiveness opened the way for a new chapter in their relationship.

A Story of Oleg, a man in his early forties:

"I'm happily married. Two kids (ages 12 and 10). My wife and I are both believers now, though we both had wild years as young people. We met each other in a rehab center for drug addicts. Fifteen years ago, after overcoming our addictions and completing the program, we got married. Yet, last week, I got a phone call from a 20-year-old daughter I never knew I had. She moved to our city for university and wants to meet me. What should I do?"

"Were you surprised to find out about her?" I asked.

"To be honest, no, because I always knew there was a good chance I had fathered more children. Especially since my friend's circle during that time was very narrow. I knew in those open relationships some women had abortions, some decided to have children. I didn't think much about it, because it was often hard to figure out who was the father. I had sex with those who were sleeping around."

"If you're thinking about establishing paternity through genetic testing, I don't recommend it. Whether she is your

biological daughter or not is not the main question here. I don't share the nostalgia about "blood relations". A biological father is not a dad if he is not part of his child's life. If the mother of this girl never filed for child support or asked for your involvement in this girl's upbringing, it means she accepted the principle of you not taking the role of a father."

"It happened exactly as you said. The girl's mother got married and they built a good life for themselves. Her husband turned out to be a very decent person and he adopted the child. She called him "dad".

"So, throughout her life this girl had a father who lived in her world, cared for her mom and their family, and raised her. This man provided your biological daughter with care and gave her a family. And now, she shows up eager to restore the "family bond with her " real" dad?"

"Yes. That is exactly what she said, 'restore her connection with her "real father". I guess some family specialist led her to this idea."

"You shouldn't call her "daughter". This is my first recommendation. She's not your daughter, and you're not her father. Don't support this young woman's disappointing attitude toward her family"

"So, she's a stranger to me?"

"Yes. Just as you are to her."

"Should I meet with her at all?"

"Why not? But not as a guilty 'dad.' Meet her to ask forgiveness for all the men (including yourself) whose recklessness and irresponsibility brought chaos into the lives of many children out of wedlock. As a result, many missed out on the father's love, and many would not be given a chance to be born. Not everyone is as lucky as this girl, who had a good dad in her mother's husband."

"From my understanding, she expects financial help from me and wants to stay with us."

"On what grounds? As a daughter?"

"Yeah. She told me that as soon as she found out her real dad, that's me, had abandoned her, everything inside her shattered. She broke up with the boyfriend because of the pain she went through deep inside. She fought with her parents pretending to be a real family. And she is here now, staying temporarily at a hotel. My wife doesn't want her to move in with us. My wife calls the girl's behavior emotional blackmail and 'a sudden fatherhood for convenience.'"

"Your wife is right. This girl wants you to play her game and make you a scape goat for all the hard times in her life she is causing herself. But she is the one who is responsible for the choices she makes: lies, manipulation, grudges, accusations, contempt, and betrayal of her parents. She chose to play the victim where everyone owes her everything and she invites you to play with her. The choice is yours, whether to play along or stay honest.

"You sound exactly like my wife when you mention manipulation".

"Thank God for your wise wife. Tell her you are sorry for the pain you caused by letting this young woman's manipulations threaten your family. Ask your children to forgive you for the wild youth with many addictions and sexual freedom, when you separated the pleasure from responsibility, neglecting the impact on the women involved and the children who might have come from those choices. Let this situation be a lesson for you and your kids, and this girl.

"So, how should I act when I am around this girl when we meet?"

"The main thing, as I've said already, don't fall for her "real dad" games. Her father is not you, but the man who raised her. And she tried to replace him, repaying her parents for the life they gave her with resentment and hatred. You can help her, but not as a "newfound daddy" she wants you to be, but as a wise mentor. Get rid of lies and manipulation. If you give in to guilt and shame she wants to impose on you, she may lose any chance to return to family values."

I will give you a quick update on Oleg's story. He handled this challenge with dignity. On the same day after our talk, he and his wife called the mother of this "newly discovered daughter." The woman was very thankful when she heard from them, because this twenty-year-old had left their house, withdrawing a large sum of money from her father's bank account. It turned out that in recent years she started using drugs, became very disrespectful toward her parents and aggressive toward her younger siblings. During a household discussion, the decision was made to move her into her college dorm.

Oleg and his wife met with the girl, offered mentorship and an opportunity to build a friendly connection, but she didn't listen. Her goal was to become a part of their family and totally abandon the real one where she belonged. Throughout the conversation, she relied heavily on accusations and emotional appeals for sympathy. When she realized Oleg wasn't buying into her narrative, she lashed out with aggression and even attempted to use lawyers to blackmail them—but her efforts ultimately failed. The young girl had no other choice but to return home. She went back to college, moved into her dorm, and apologized to her parents. I don't know what happened to her afterwards, but I sincerely hope that her apology was genuine and that she was able to stop being a "prodigal daughter" and restore her relationship with her family.

...Once at a youth conference where I spoke about forgiveness, I had a conversation with a **young 26-year-old guy who was left as a newborn:**

"I will never forgive my mother! She left me in the hospital after I was born. She was the reason I was deprived of family and a normal childhood. The first twenty years of my life were hell: orphanages for babies and kids, crime, betrayal, and jail. Then a miracle happened to me. While I was in jail, I came to know the Lord, found new values and my life's purpose, and experienced a rebirth. I got back on my feet, now I have my own business and a family of my own. God taught me how to love, though I thought I would never trust or love a

woman. And now out of the blue, my biological mother finds me and asks me to forgive her. She feels bad and ashamed about what she did. But how can I forgive her?"

From a human perspective, it's incredibly difficult. Such pain doesn't simply vanish. The scars linger and they ache. Yet in truth, the path forward is narrow. There are only two choices.

Choice one: Continue nursing bitterness and resentment, clinging stubbornly to the prison of unforgiveness by locking yourself inside and throwing away the key, denying freedom and joy. All the while, obsessively seeking to punish the mother through silence, blame, and the weight of guilt you refuse to release.

Option two: Forgive. Naturally, it's important to understand her reasons for wanting to rekindle the relationship. If it's just for her son's money, then provide her with minimal financial support according to the Fifth Commandment. But if her repentance is genuine, there is a tremendous opportunity to rebuild a relationship, one that could become a blessing not only for her, but for the entire family, especially the children.

Why some people refuse to forgive

Have you ever wondered why some people *prefer* to stay stuck in unforgiveness and resentment?

Because it's easier.

When you don't forgive, you owe no one anything. You get to live with the mindset that the world owes *you*. It's easy to blame everything for the pain you carry. Unforgiveness produces the illusion of power over the person whom you accuse.

Those who refuse to forgive often anchor themselves to familiar slogans:

"My trauma is too deep to forgive." Really? What exactly do you gain by being held hostage by toxic emotions like shame, guilt, bitterness, or fear? What does true healing from unforgiveness look like? Do you recover your emotional stability by partaking in the same old poison every day?

"I have to teach them a lesson, so they'll feel guilty." Are you sure certain you're stepping into the right role? Do you truly believe you have the moral authority to reshape people, including your parents into an image you deemed ideal? Do you consider yourself wiser than God?

"If I forgive, they'll just do it again." Forgiveness isn't about controlling the other person's behavior. It's about gaining freedom and peace in your own heart. Carrying the burden of someone else's choices is exhausting. Forgiving doesn't mean pretending nothing's happened. Forgiveness doesn't mean automatic restoration of your relationship.

"They hurt me; now let them suffer too. Someone must punish them!" But it works vice versa. When you don't forgive, you're stuck in a prison of your negative emotions. You spend your energy avoiding the person who hurt you, dodging being in the same group, the same room, the same project. You force yourself not to think about them. And guess what? You're losing your own freedom. You end up punishing yourself.

"If I forgive, they'll think I am weak and deserve to be hurt" It is not true, because only *strong* people know how to forgive and are ready to forgive. A strong person doesn't let anyone mistreat them. They are fully aware that compassion isn't the same thing as enabling toxic behavior. And it works vice versa: in the process of forgiving you get rid of poisonous emotions and become stronger

"I don't want them to think they 'won' the argument" The person who is able to forgive is the real winner. Forgiveness restores their health, brings peace of mind, and freedom from poison-filled feelings. On the other hand, the one who refuses to forgive keeps stacking up bitterness and their ego starts feeding fake self-importance.

You always have a choice:

* to forgive or to stay bitter,

* to bless or to curse,

* to show gratitude or to stew in complaints,

* to get healthy (physical, emotional, and spiritual) or become sick.

A person who refuses to forgive is often lonely and miserable.

A forgiving person, on the other hand, is kind and magnetic.

Resentment: A Common Phenomenon with Profound Consequences

Let's look at some interesting theories from researchers who explore the phenomenon of resentment in the field of classical psychology.

Fritz Perls, founder of Gestalt therapy, called resentment *the worst form of "unfinished business"* — or what is also known as an *"open gestalt"*.

In Gestalt therapy, these terms refer to the core reasons behind a person's mental and emotional instability. So, when it comes to the dilemma *"should I forgive or stay offended?"*, classic Gestalt therapy has a clear answer: **forgive.**

In his research and therapy sessions, Perls emphasized techniques that help a person develop a **whole, integrated self** across five areas of life:

- Physical

- Emotional

- Intellectual

- Social

- Spiritual

Perls believed that mental health comes from harmony in these areas, when we live in tune with our bodies, feelings, thoughts, people, and values.

In his works he defined three zones of awareness:

> **The middle zone** — your inner dialogue, imagination, assumptions, and overthinking;

> **The inner zone** — real, current emotions and bodily experiences;

> **The outer zone** — events and things happening around, the outside world;

According to Perls, people develop **neuroses and psychological problems** when they get stuck in the *middle zone*, where they find themselves overanalyzing, fantasizing, or going over grudges repeatedly. And they end up disconnecting from their true feelings and reality.

He believed that a person can't move forward if they live in the past, stuck in what "should have been," playing old drama over in their mind, or choosing to view life through the lens of their *resentments*. This disconnect prevents healing and growth of the mind and building healthy relationships.

N.Y. Gusakov sees *resentment* as a destructive way of defending your own sense of worth.

From his perspective, people tend to create an image of their "self-worth" and then they cling to resentment to protect that image.

When your *ego-based worth* becomes your top value and you have no other way to feel validated, you end up trapped in a cycle of emotional defense. You feel that you are always easily disrespected or dismissed, and these feelings lead you to resentment as a tool for defending your "worth".

Shifting from ego-worth to personal dignity is the way out of this never-ending cycle, according to Gusakov. You stop viewing yourself solely through the lens of a self-constructed image and begin to see yourself through the richness of real relationships, honest conversations, and shared human experience.

As a result, resentment slowly fades.

Gusakov points to a higher form of dignity called *human dignity*. Here you start recognizing the value of being human not because of status, control, or self-representation, but because we're made in the image of God, created with meaning and purpose. Embracing your *human dignity* frees you from obsession over recognition and prevents you from falling into insecurities. You gain the ability to build strong connections and healthy relationships, to love and to forgive, and to live your life free of bitterness. You stop destroying your life and your relationships with people and with God through resentment.

Gusakov's views align with thinkers from existential psychology like Søren Kierkegaard, Viktor Frankl, Karl Jaspers, B. Bratus, and others.

David Myers looks at resentment through the lens of *"memory construction."* He says our memory of the past isn't fixed. It is formed by how we currently feel about people and situations from the past. In a long-term study of married couples, researchers asked the newlyweds on their wedding day questions about how they felt about each other. Fifteen years later they were asked the same exact questions. What they discovered was fascinating:

With couples who stayed together and built a healthy relationship:

* Their memories of each other became *more positive* over time.

* They strengthened their positive view of their spouse and their wedding day.

With couples who had divorced or constantly fighting in their marriage:

* Their memories flipped.

* Things they once thought were beautiful and meaningful now felt fake. "That was all a lie," "It was manipulation," "I should've seen the red flags."

In Myers's point of view, **we rewrite the past** *to match our current emotional state.*

These insights from social psychologist David Myers align with the core conclusions of the classic thinkers from the dynamic schools of psychology — C.G. Jung, Alfred Adler, Sigmund Freud, and Erich Fromm, as we've discussed earlier.

Dr. Don Colbert, in his work on emotional health, puts *resentment* into the category as he calls it *"deadly emotions."*

These emotions, he says, are not just mentally toxic; they are physically dangerous.

They can trigger a wide range of psychosomatic illnesses by disrupting the body's internal balance.

When someone holds on to resentment, their health pays the price. Neurologists, endocrinologists, psychotherapists, and clinical psychologists are very familiar with this concept as they regularly deal with psychosomatic symptoms that trace back to buried emotional pain.

In many cases, resentment is not just a contributing factor to an illness, but it's the root cause.

Studies show that the list of stress-related illnesses keeps growing. Among them:

- Asthma

- Coronary heart disease

- Tachycardia

- Heart attack

- Rheumatoid arthritis

- Migraine and headache

- Thyroid problems

...and many others.

Our emotional state is deeply connected to how our brain functions.

When your sense of well-being is threatened, the limbic system, the brain's emotional control center, triggers one of three responses:

- **Flight** – You run. Not just physically, but emotionally. You might escape into addiction (drugs, porn, social media…), or fake illnesses, or just *slam the door and disappear* from relationships or responsibilities.

- **Freeze** – You shut down. You bury your feelings deep, suppress your emotions; over time, that internal pressure turns into physical illness.

- **Fight** – You lash out. You stop caring about what is right or wrong. You attack others or turn that aggression inward (that's called *self-harm*, and it can take the form of cutting, destructive behavior, even suicide).

Resentment can completely hijack someone's behavior. A resentful person isn't just emotionally miserable. They can be *dangerous* to themselves and to others. Granted, not every grudge leads to suicide; however, unresolved resentment lies behind most suicides.

Looking at the criminal stats, we see that a large percentage of crimes committed "in the heat of the moment" are fueled by unresolved bitterness; domestic crimes often carry a level of cruelty that's deeply personal.

"Is it truly possible to live without taking offense?"

Resentment is an emotion that, like any other, arises beyond our conscious desire or control. It's crucial to understand that we cannot directly control emotions, as we can't control other processes within the limbic system of our brain. But we can and should control our actions. There is a key difference between a reaction of the limbic system, and a conscious, intentional action. The latter involves resolving emotional pain, while the former functions like a temporary pain-reliever.

"Train your senses to discern good from evil", and "Be transformed by the renewing of your mind", these profound words were written nearly 2,000 years ago in the Bible, long before today's research in neurophysiology and neuropsychology. Yes, we can't prevent emotions from building up. But through actions and deliberate choices rooted in love, care, forgiveness, and gratitude, we can reshape the neural pathways responsible for our emotional responses. In other words, you can train your emotional reflexes the same way you'd train your muscles through habit, repetition, and conscious decision-making.

There's a well-known proverb that says:

"Sow a habit, reap a character. Sow a character, reap a destiny."

This ancient truth resonates deeply with modern psychology, especially in the **cognitive-behavioral** approach, which teaches that our repeated thoughts and actions form who we become.

B.F. Skinner, the founder of operant conditioning and one of the key voices of the *first wave* of cognitive behavioral therapy (CBT), believed that personality isn't a deep inner mystery but it's a collection of learned behaviors, shaped by the experiences we pick up throughout our life. Skinner argued that a person's actions and relationships are driven less by inner emotions and more by **external reinforcement** from the environment.

In other words: we do what we've been trained to do, especially if we benefit from it.

For example, if a 19-year-old drops out of college and becomes a waiter we can ask "Why?" According to Skinner, the answer is simple: because this decision has *benefits*:

- No more early mornings.

- No more boring professors or lectures.

- Financial independence and freedom to move out and live on your own terms.

- Possibility to party all night "with my buddies and hook up with whoever I want to".

According to Skinner that decision isn't necessarily rooted in some tragic childhood trauma or emotional wounds. Skinner would say that this decision is strictly behavior driven by the perceived reward. Skinner proposed that to effectively support individuals in facing life's challenges, therapists should empower them to become their own therapists—capable of identifying destructive behavioral patterns and replacing them with constructive alternatives.

Aaron Beck, the founder of the *second wave of* CBT, shifted the focus from behavior to **thoughts**.

He believed distorted thinking — not just actions — is at the root of most emotional struggles. Backed by research, Beck showed that it's not what *happens* to us that causes emotional pain, but how we *interpret* those events. In conclusion, he aligns with many psychodynamic thinkers. From his perspective, the role of the therapist is to assist someone in recognizing how their thoughts could be misleading and then help the individual to reframe those thoughts. When that shift occurs, emotions naturally follow.

Both **Skinner** and **Beck** emphasize one key principle: personal responsibility.

They believe that real change starts when a person consciously chooses healthier patterns in behavior, in thinking, and especially in relationships. Until a person becomes aware that even their destructive patterns serve some hidden desire, they remain stuck in these patterns. No transformation is possible until you recognize that the so-called "benefit" of your current patterns is what's holding you back.

Take Andrew for example. He's over forty and still holding on to a "childhood wound" from thirty-two years ago.

He and his mom were at a seaside resort. He got sick and had a fever. One morning he woke up and next to a ripe mango he saw a note that said:

"I went for a swim. I will be back before you wake up. If not, please enjoy this mango, I'll be back soon. Love you, my sweet boy!"

Andrew cried his heart out, and guess what? He still cries every time he tells his tragic tale. (Back in the day, in Russia, parents could leave their children alone and many did so.)

He didn't even remember the mango at first because the bitterness lingered.

He didn't mention that his mother had two jobs for a year to have an opportunity to take her son to this seaside resort in the summer. But all he remembered was his "bad mom" who dared to leave him alone to go swimming.

And now he goes back to the same old story anytime he wants to justify his personal failures:

- *his dysfunctional marriage ("with this childhood trauma, I just can't love"),*

- *his envy of a successful older brother ("my brother was my mom's favorite"),*

- *his constant job-hopping ("every boss is a fool, and all co-workers are suck-ups and my soul can't bear it"),*

- *his inflated ego ("how can a soul this pure survive in such a dirty world?")*

It was the Healing Sandwich technique that led him to change by drawing him into a place of gratefulness, forgiveness, and tender care.

Let's look at Elena, in her 30s, who with bitterness constantly blames her own parents for everything, as she seeks approval from the family of her abusive husband. Looking through her childhood photos, we see a house with a garden, her parents, three older brothers, family trips to the zoo, vacations at the sea, birthdays surrounded by loving grandparents, aunts, and uncles. Nothing in these pictures aligns with the venom of her current blame-game.

She married a handsome truck driver against her parents' advice. She refused to see all the red flags. And there were many: drug use during his teenage years and occasional use meantime, multiple women, and a couple of children out of wedlock. There was a history of mental illness on his mother's side, a cheating father, and both of his parents were heavy drinkers. He was aggressive and very jealous. As a result, her life today is burdened by marital and emotional challenges:

- *an unemployed, and depressed husband who criticizes her about her age, looks, housekeeping, lack of "adventure" in the bedroom.*

- *a low-paid teaching job at school with "bratty kids and rude parents,"*

- *a mother-in-law begging for cash to sober up,*

- *a father-in-law who shows up at family events with random girlfriends,*

- *a teenage daughter who says, "Our family sucks."*

Digging up old "traumas" and blaming her mom and dad is an emotional painkiller for her because her real life is a slow-burning disaster.

Facing the truth would mean admitting:

- "I walked into this mess deliberately with my eyes half-closed under the influence of toxic emotions"

- "I'm in an abusive relationship which I chose, and not my mom and dad."

- "My husband became the center of my universe, and I let him do it because it keeps me grounded in my resentment."

- "My life is my responsibility"

Acknowledging the truth was hard for her; it is always hard. It is easier to continue blaming someone else, using that as an emotional *anesthetic* for resentment and self-pity.

On the other hand, facing the truth would mean facing *her own role* in cutting off the people from her life who truly loved her. It would mean admitting that she took emotions as a foundation for her decisions, not reality:

"I *felt that* my husband is the only one who needs me…"

"I *sensed* that my parents betrayed me…"

"It *seemed* that my mom has been always trying to control me…"

Elena's recovery began with letting go of an idea that her emotions were sacred.

She had spent years believing that her feelings: resentment, guilt, and fear must never be discredited. Hyper-focusing on her emotions blinded her.

At the very first session she reached consensus that several emotions aren't meant to be cherished. Shame, fear, bitterness, and blame should not be safeguarded. She needs to *challenge these emotions* and reject and stop manipulation from traumatic memories and emotional stress.

Elena put an end to it all when she realized how one gets hooked endlessly digging in one's wounds.

… You show up in crisis to a session being overwhelmed, depressed, and emotionally depleted. You are asked to talk about your childhood and uncovering old tales starts - about your mom being cold, and your dad being absent; then suddenly, everything starts to make sense to you in your mind.

"Wow! I totally forgot about that! And now I can totally see — *that's* what messed me up!"

Your brain jumps in to help you. It retrieves every painful memory it can find, neutralizes the happy ones and adds more bitter tones to match the mood you're in today. Instantly, the blame zeroes in on- mom, dad and the past. It *feels* like a breakthrough, or a release. In fact, it is nothing more than an emotional painkiller in the form of a "self-righteous" anger. You are now prosecutor, judge, and victim. You feel liberated and powerful.

"Finally, I see that I've been mistreated."

Time passed after the session, the high fades away, and all the pain finds its way back. Thus, you go back for another doze of an emotional painkiller. You uncover more pain, and as a result you get another temporary release. You're not healing in this repetitive cycle—you're deepening the pain, creating even more to unpack. You're not *healing your wounds-* you're *nurturing* your pain.

Resentment is adhesive by nature—anchored in unresolved pain

Resentment finds its way into your thoughts, your relationships, and your sense of meaning.

Resentment distorts how you see the world.

Resentment keeps "childhood trauma diggers" in business.

And this could go on forever if you do not get rid of resentment. That is where good specialist can help you.

In academic circles, the term "happiness" hasn't gained popularity, and often is replaced with synonyms like "psychological well-being" or "subjective well-being". These terms mean the level of how good your life *feels* to you. Let's be honest: a life rooted in resentment would not feel good at all.

This phenomenon has been explored from many angles by researchers like A. Maslow, C. Rogers, G. Allport, C. G. Jung, E. Erikson, M. Jahoda, and others.

I will focus on the **theory by Carol Ryff.** This theory synthesized insights from many thinkers and defined six core components of psychological well-being: **self-acceptance, positive**

relationships with others, autonomy, environmental mastery, purpose in life, and personal growth.

- **Self-acceptance** reflects a positive evaluation of oneself and one's life as a whole—a willingness to embrace both strengths and weaknesses.

  This includes the shift from what we earlier called "ego-centered dignity" to "personal dignity" and finally to "human dignity": recognizing your value as rooted in transcendent, God-given principles highlighted both in Scripture and in the works of psychological luminaries like Jaspers, Frankl, Rogers, and Jung.

- **Positive relationships with others** involve empathy and openness to connection.

  Genuine openness is impossible if you can't accept criticism, and if you're unwilling to apologize, or if you are unwilling to forgive, instead, they hold onto the resentment.

- **Autonomy** means the ability to think independently, even when your views differ from the majority.

  It's also about discerning wheat from weeds, universal values from trendy nonsense.

- **Environmental mastery** is the ability to shape your surroundings to meet your needs and overcome obstacles on the path to your goals.

  This includes managing the relationships you're involved in - in marriage, in friendships, at work, and as parent-child.

- **Personal growth** involves a desire to develop and eagerness to learn.
  What is important: "new" doesn't only mean the latest hype; it can be rediscovering timeless truths that humanity has cherished for decades, centuries, even millennia.

- **Purpose in life** gives meaning to our existence and allows you to understand and embrace your past, live fully in the present, and anticipate the future with hope.

Resentment and unforgiveness don't fit into any part of psychological well-being

Instead, they lead to emotional and social problems, and behavior issues.

Resentment makes everything look worse than it is, wrecking your inner peace.

During my workshops, I often use the metaphor of "Cup of Subjective Well-Being" to demonstrate how emotional destruction unfolds.

- Imagine a "Cup of Subjective Well-Being" filled with all the good stuff we talked about earlier: self-acceptance, purpose, growth, etc.

Picture 1.

- Now, resentment (a conscious grudge) is like a heavy substance sinking to the bottom of the cup.

Picture 2.

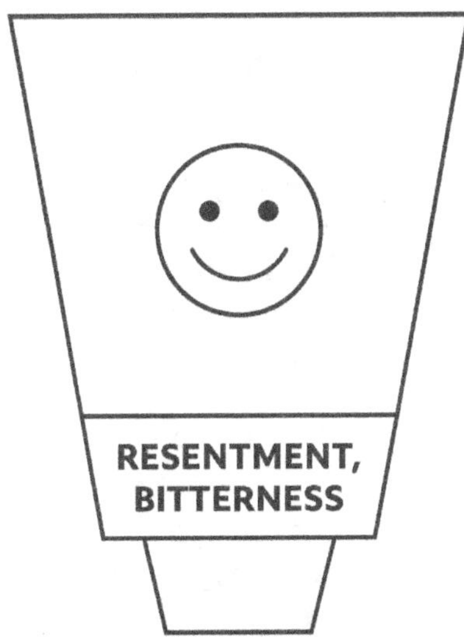

- This grudge forces you to look for a scapegoat to blame, fuels desire for revenge, and stirs up other toxic emotions like fear, shame, and guilt.

Picture 3.

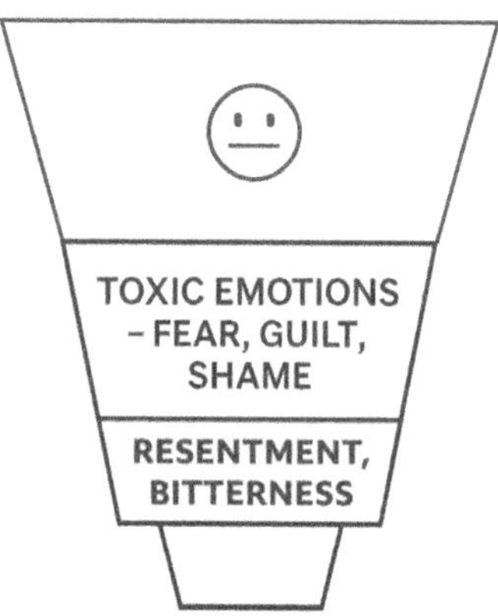

Pay close attention to how there's less room left in the cup for well-being as this substance sink

- Next comes anxiety, which can turn into chronic stress.

Picture 4.

Too much negativity in your mind leads to serious psychological and behavioral problems: no positive feelings, physical symptoms like headaches or stomachaches, sleep troubles, irritability, depression, trouble focusing, poor eating habits, loss of sexual desire, addictive behaviors, chronic fatigue, aggression, and even self-harm...

Picture 5.

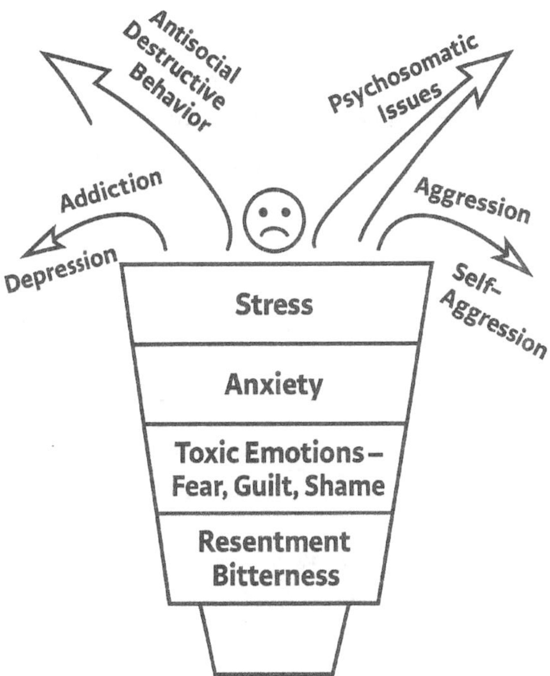

It is pointless to start your healing process by "turning off" stress, because anxiety, fear, aggression, and grudges will still be there. It's like turning on the faucet of stress without ever shutting off the main valve.

Picture 6.

You can get a brief relief, and a handful of negativity flows out. However, most of it stays in and quickly rebuilds itself.

Approaching emotional work through the lens of fear, guilt, and shame also cannot help you. You will receive only temporary relief because the root cause remains untouched.

The faucet should be opened at the level of your resentment.

Picture 7

In this case all the" crap" pours out of the "cup", and then it can be transformed into "fertilizer". As a result, the "cup" can be filled again with all the ingredients of psychological well-being: **self-acceptance, positive relationships with others, autonomy, environmental mastery, purpose in life, and personal growth.**

The Healing Sandwich method is very helpful in this process.

In my training program for married couples, which consists of 12 sessions held individually and in a closed-group format, we focus on cultivating marital intimacy through a range of essential skills. These include conflict resolution, identifying triggers of dissatisfaction, and planning for a fulfilling and prosperous married life. We also address key areas such as financial and sexual well-being and explore the dynamics of relationships with children and parents.

During our Sessions 3 and 4 we start our deep work on resentment. Many people experience resistance. We also witness extremes—some couples become visibly overwhelmed when asked to write down all their resentment since the beginning of their relationship. One piece of paper, even in the smallest print, is not long enough. Others leave the page blank, claiming, "It's all been forgiven a long time ago." However, according to the subjective well-being questionnaire we use, perfect well-being has rarely been observed.

One husband explained his reluctance to "open the faucet" by saying: "If I do, all that crap will pour out! It will smell badly! Why would I do that?"

And here we face a choice. We can

EITHER choose to live with that "toxic waste" blocking the perspectives for relationship growth, personal development, self-acceptance, and all the other ingredients of our well-being.

OR we can choose to "drain it out," turning that "carp into a fertilizer", restoring the ingredients of the "Subjective Well-Being Cup"

In Conclusion

To free yourself from the triggers of neurosis, depression, aggression/self-harm, and other psychological burdens, start with getting rid of resentment

Chapter Seven

THE POWER OF THE EXTENDED FAMILY

One day, I received a video from a person requesting my comments. A woman was confidently stating:

> *"Once you turn 18, you no longer have a family. You are now just a man or a woman, until you marry. Because family means husband, wife, and children."*

Sadly, the notion of 'age-based orphanhood' is echoed far too often now.

It is important to underscore several fundamental flaws inherent in this approach.

First, these specialists often omit crucial context—their statements stem from an extremely individualistic worldview.

Second, the term "family" is not limited to spouses and their children. There is more than one layer to a family structure:

- **Marriage (husband and wife)**

- **Nuclear family (parents and their children)**

- **Extended family (in-laws, grandparents)**

- **Kinship family (including all relatives—cousins, aunts, uncles, etc.)**

Third, the need to belong to a community of people is a fundamental human need. The more of these healthy communities you belong to, the stronger your psychological well-being becomes. Your well-being in any community depends on the quality of the relationships in your primary one—your family (in all layers).

Today the word "separation" has become a mantra, a "sacred cow" that everyone is expected to worship, or they become an enemy of all humanity and/or their own children.

A meme has been circulating online that captures this mindset perfectly:

A goofy-looking character—maybe the cartoonish bug-eyed guy, a clueless donkey, or a bewildered frog—stands under the caption:

> *"You messed things up with a psychologist, now you have no friends, no family, but hey, you have personal boundaries and your unwavering point of view."*

I don't like the term "separation" because these pseudo-experts have turned it into a pathological absolute.

Those who talk about such kind of "separation" call for:

- severing close ties with parents;

- rejecting kinship ties;

- erasing or forgetting your past;

- turning away from important people while hurting their feelings.

- dismissing the feelings and needs of your loved ones.

Some even publish lists of *"perfect separation behaviors"*: "call your mom no more than once a month", "never help your parents financially or give them a hand around the house", "abandon old family traditions and anniversaries" …

In contrast to this distortion, I prefer talking about **creating a separate family system**—an important developmental milestone when two people marry and form their own household, separate from their parents.

What does it mean to "create a separate family system"?

Let me provide an illustration:

Two people get married.

In their new family system, there are two people.

Then, they have their first child (e.g. let it be a daughter) Now there are three people in the system.

Later, they have a son—four people in their system.

When their grown-up child - a daughter, gets married, the family system returns to three, but nearby there are two more family systems — the daughter's and in-laws. Each system has its own head (husband), its own hostess (wife), its own traditions and rules — but they are all family – an extended one. They are all connected as **relatives**.

> *We experienced this firsthand, when our eldest daughter got married: there were many more birthdays; the dinner tables grew longer to seat the whole family, and our three family systems — ours, our in-law's, and our daughter's — became close and dear.*

It is meant to happen this way, when parents bless and let their children go off to build new families.

An unhealthy example of this dynamic is when, at a wedding, mother says in her speech, "I always dreamed of having a son, and now I finally have one—my daughter married one!"

This mindset is deeply misguided. You do not gain a son; you set your daughter free, so she and her husband can build their separate family life together. Once they succeed, the time will come when they will no longer say, *"my mom"*/ *"his dad."* Instead, they will call their parents "our *moms*" and *"our dads"*.

The same process should happen as each child leaves home.

The opposite unhealthy example is when the newly born spouses cuts themselves from their kinship family.

Nowadays, what we often see looks more like a parody. It's like that viral animated ad where a leather-clad biker— *"YOUR PSYCHOLOGIST*—roars in on a motorcycle, scoops up a bearded man tagged «*YOU*" and speeds off into the unknown. Meanwhile, the man's stunned relatives cry out in confusion,

"You can't just cut us off! We're your family!"—and the man nonchalantly flips them off.

As for me, I have a few questions for the bearded man:

> Where exactly is "your psychologist" taking you?

> To his own family?

> Will he replace your "toxic" relatives with the new ones and become your ideal loving family?

> What lesson is he teaching you by doing this? Are you going to call him whenever life gets tough?

> Is he teaching you to continue disrespecting your family with vulgar gestures?

> Is this how you are going to spend the rest of your life and develop your children in such relations with family?

> And isn't it perfect for the person who called himself "your psychologist" to keep charging you for unpacking your "childhood wounds" if you are willing to pay for this service?

During my premarital counseling sessions, one of the hottest topics I raise is: *"How will your relationship with your parents change after the wedding?"*

The answers usually reveal two extremes:

- *"Not at all."*

- *"Completely."*

The first group resists forming their own family system. The second group tries to erase their parents from their lives. Both options are harmful.

Before marriage, each person lives by the rules and traditions set and observed by their immediate family balancing their own interests with those of their close families. After they become a couple, they have to decide how to proceed:

* Which family traditions will we keep, and to what extent?

* How will our relatives fit into our new priorities and plans?

In other words, marriage demands a shift from a "roommate thinking" (cohabitation) to marital thinking (one life for two people, "one flesh"). Let me give you an example.

In cohabitation:

"These are my friends, those are yours"

"This is my money, that's yours"

"This is my car, that's yours"

"This is my phone, that's yours"

"These are my responsibilities; those are yours."

In marriage:

It's all OURS—our friends, our money (both partners have equal access), our household responsibilities and parenting, our phones (no passwords kept from each other).

In cohabitation:

"If you do that again, I'm moving back with my mom!"

"If you don't like it, let's just get divorced."

In marriage:

"We understand that we are one life, one flesh. We must resolve conflicts together and, if needed, we will seek help (from our friends, parents, professionals, pastors) because we are both responsible for this relationship."

In cohabitation:

"This is my mom, that's your mom. These are my relatives, those are yours."

In marriage:

"THESE are OUR parents, OUR relatives."

In cohabitation:

"This is my life, that's your life. This is my personal space—don't cross my boundaries, and I won't cross yours."

In marriage:

> "ONE LIFE FOR TWO", "one flesh"—shared space and shared time."

Why Severing Relationships Isn't Always the Best Solution

Serious psychological problems often emerge in families where one or both spouses buy into the illusion of "we are both traumatized and we will heal each other," or "we don't need anyone; we must cut ties with our families"

It adds fuel to the fire until the toxic emotions eventually explode in the «Subjective Well-Being Cup" (see chapter 6). Unresolved issues with close relationships from the past block solving new problems. A person who neglects relationships in their first (parental) family and/or living with resentment, has lots of problems in building healthy relationships in the marriage.

This offers a wide range of landscapes for applying the Healing Sandwich method in the family.

Today's flood of separators all seems to be stuck on repeating:

> *"If you care for your parents, your children will suffer."*

> *"Your kids get neglected, because you spend too much time looking after your parents and not your kids."*

> *"Energy flows down, not up—so you owe your kids but not your parents, and your parents owe you for life."*

All these slogans ignore (or deliberately deny) the timeless laws of love:

✓ The more you give, the more you receive.

✓ The more you invest, the deeper your love grows.

✓ The stronger your marriage, the more love your children will experience.

✓ The healthier your extended family relationships, the more love and support your nuclear family will get—including from your parents.

The "Five Refrigerators Rule"

I once heard a fascinating presentation about "Five Refrigerators Rule"

The main idea is:

* If a child under the age of 10 has **five refrigerators** in their life, then as a teenager, they are far less likely to struggle with antisocial behavior, addictions, depression, or suicidal tendencies.

* By contrast, children who grow up with only **one refrigerator** face a much higher risk of falling into above mentioned problems (up to 85%).

What is a "refrigerator"? It's a metaphor for any home where a child knows they will always be welcomed, fed, given a place to sleep, looked after, where parents can be substituted when necessary.

Let's count your "fridges".

> The first refrigerator is your parents' home.

> The second and third are the grandparents' homes (with three refrigerators, the risks already drop significantly—three out of five kids to avoid the danger zone.)

> Add more refrigerators for great-grandparents, aunts, uncles; you can take a deep breath—those teenage years might go more smoothly than you expect.

This concept does not invent anything new. It simply expresses metaphorically what anthropology and ethnopsychology have known for decades: in collectivist cultures, where extended families are woven tightly into everyday life, adolescent crises are far less common than in individualistic cultures, where the nuclear family (*husband, wife, kids*) reigns supreme.

But Then People Say…

> "You do not know my mom! She is always criticizing my husband and talks behind his back."

> "My mother-in-law cannot stand me. I never want to visit her, and I rarely let her see my kids."

Whenever I hear this—especially when they toss in the word "toxic"—my reaction is straightforward: if you say you love your children, then do it for their sake—turn the homes of your parents and relatives into those very "refrigerators" of safety and belonging.

What is important: it's not enough to "allow a short visit" or drop by "under your supervision and total control because "all grandmas are clueless/toxic/foolish/unskilled at raising kids😵"

No, the home of a relative member becomes a *true refrigerator* only when your child can be there without you and your interference into that home's system

> Do Grandma and Grandpa live far away? Let your child stay with them for a few weeks each year and now there is a refrigerator.

> You leave your kids to spend the night with relatives once a month (**without you**)? That is also a refrigerator.

It is important to remember one principle: YOU NEVER DICTATE YOUR RULES TO OTHER HOUSEHOLDS

The best socialization for kids happens precisely within various family structures when each has its own rules, customs, and traditions. In these different environments, your child learns not only to feel loved wherever they go, but also to love others and adapt gracefully.

"What if My Mom Doesn't Like When We Visit"

Guess what? It's on you to become a guest who is welcome.

It is no wonder that your parents do not exactly roll out the red carpet if:

- you barge in with an attitude "We are coming and we are starving!"

- you carry layers of unspoken judgment toward your parents' way of life, you constantly tell them how to live and what to do in their own home

- you control what your child *should* or *shouldn't* eat/do/ say in their households!

Start fixing your mistakes with small, intentional steps. I am going to give you a very simple but practical life-hack which has been successfully used by families in cases when they used not to be highly welcomed in other homes, including grannies:

You make a phone call: "Mom, I'm calling to see if we with children can stop by for 15 minutes tonight? We want to hang out for a bit, then we'll be on our way."

If she says yes, show up with her favorite sushi rolls, Dad's favorite drink, and disposable plates, so no one must clean up after you. After hugs and kisses, set the table quickly, enjoy your little meal together, and then, exactly after 15 minutes, get up and say:

"It is time to go!"

Make sure to clear the table and put everything away.

Even if your parents say, "Why are you leaving so soon?!" you reply:

"We told you we'll drop by for only 15 minutes, but we'll come by again soon, right kids? Give Grandma and Grandpa kisses!"

Next week, do the same for 40 minutes...

I'm confident that after a while, when you ask if you can leave the kids with them for two hours (maybe even days) while you run some errands, they are most likely to say YES.

Why?

- You've built the reputation of being a considerate and responsible guest.

- Your kids now understand the *dos and don'ts* in grannies' house.

   The sooner you start, the better — especially before your kids reach their teenage years. You will notice positive changes in your kids' behaviors before long.

In my practice, I've seen dozens of cases where children's neuroses, phobias, and anxiety disorders melted away simply because their parents rebuilt relationships with the relatives and created these "refrigerators" of love and security.

"Do Friends Count as Refrigerators?" – the common question I get when we talk about the "refrigerator rule".

Only if you have solid prolonging friendship and often spend time together on a regular basis only for kids under age six. But in general, friends don't have the same responsibility as relatives when it comes to supporting a child at crucial times in life, when someone must step into the role of a parent.

An extended family is an unmatched safety net. When there is a crisis—signs of abuse, infidelity, addiction, health problems—it's usually the extended family that becomes the most effective and natural support group.

That is why the usual practice in family or crisis consulting is to map out family ties as one of the first steps. The stronger and healthier these connections are, the better the chances of overcoming any crises.

A Real-Life Story: Grandma and her Teenage Grandson

"My grandson's going through a rough patch. I think my daughter and my son-in-law are too strict. He's only 14! They're almost 40—shouldn't adults be wiser and more patient? But several days ago, the situation got very bad and they kicked him out. He came to me crying."

"Did you call your daughter? Ask what happened?"

"I did call. But I didn't ask. What is there to ask? Is it ever okay to throw a child out on the street? I told my daughter as much, and she said she would rather support her husband's handling of this situation. She said I turned my grandson against them. She told me he was skipping school, smoking, being disrespectful at home, and that I should not take his side. But whose side should I be on?!"

"Obviously NOT the side of the misbehaving teenager"

"But he is just a boy! He told me what happened; it was totally his parents' fault. Several days ago, my grandson swore at his mom –my daughter… Well, you understand, cursed at her. And my son-in-law, my grandson's father, defended her, and my grandson swore at them both… The son-in-law demanded him to leave the table, but my grandson refused and said they had no right to kick him out, that he would report them to the authorities. Then the son-in-law grabbed him by the collar and threw him out the door…Tell me, is it okay to do that?"

"Your grandson, with his behavior, was he telling his father: 'Dad, please let go of me! I'm sick and tired how rude I am' That's how much your son-in-law loves his son — he did what the boy was desperately asking for!" Your poor grandson – is drowning in his own arrogance, and deep down he's desperate for boundaries."

"Are you joking?"

"Not at all."

"But what lesson does this teach the boy?!"

"A big one. First, what it means to be a man: a real man always protects the woman he loves. Second, what it means to be a son: if you're part of a family, act like a son. Don't behave like a rude tenant who doesn't even pay rent."

"But my son-in-law even threatened to take him to a boarding school, even to child services, saying, 'If that's where you

want to live, let's go fill out the paperwork.' Isn't that horrible, sending a child to foster care?!"

"Actually, your son-in-law is acting wisely. Until age 18, a minor cannot live on their own. By law, guardians are responsible for providing food, shelter, education, and ensuring a socially acceptable lifestyle. If parents fail at that, state institutions step in. Your grandson needs to understand the reality of his options. His dad's offer was a loving ultimatum—meant to snap him out of his behavior."

"I can't believe you're saying this."

"There's no magic pill to fix your grandson's attitude. Maybe that's for the best—because pills only work temporarily. True change comes when the boy himself wakes up and chooses a different path. And remember—his father said, 'Say sorry and you can come home.' That's love."

"So, what do I do?"

"What your grandson needs from you isn't a pity, He needs your strength and wisdom. Tell him: 'Don't you dare disrespect my daughter. Don't you dare talk back to your mother. Don't you dare defy your father.' You as part of his extended family should keep unity in managing this disrespectful behavior of a teenager.

The strength of an extended family is impossible to overstate—especially today, when so much "nonsense" is being preached about child-centered parenting and "gentle" approaches. For example, you've probably heard statements like:

"It's totally normal for teens to ignore and hate their parents."

"Teens are going through so much—it's natural for them to be rude."

"Teens aren't capable of managing their emotions yet."

"Teens simply reflect the dysfunction of their families."

None of that is true.

It's not true that a teenager is helpless when it comes to managing their emotions.

It's not true that every problem in a teen's life stems from their parents.

It's not true that the only "proper" way to raise them is with the "gentle, fluffy methods."

And it's certainly not true that all teens acting out are "just being normal."

So, what is the truth? **Family is a place where a teenager learns self-control and self-discipline—through healthy boundaries, discipline, and structure.**

Kids behave badly *because they're allowed to,* not because life is hard for them.

Puberty has always existed—it's been part of human existence for millennia. Only recently, due to the nonsense spread by many "trendsetters," there is an idea of the "sensitive soul in puberty" been taken to essentially giving a carte blanche for inappropriate emotion splashes and open disobedience, all under the disguise of "raising a free individual." In the process, freedom gets confused with permissiveness. The result is the opposite. This "tender psychology" leads to developing people who can not built relations, be disciplined and responsible, they are stressed being criticized and tend to practice abusive behavior covering it with mantra: "if I feel uncomfortable or upset I have right to be aggressive against those who love me".

When the extended family comes together around shared family values—care, respect for the hierarchy between children and parents, a one-life-for-two in marriage, respect to parents—children have a better chance at avoiding many risky situations and be trapped by misbehavior patterns.

Learning to Let Go (and When Not To)

More than thirty years ago, at the very start of our work providing counseling services to families, my husband and I prepared a seminar focused on the roles and dynamics of mothers- and fathers-in-law. Its core message was to equip the parents to let your adult children go? This seminar evolved over time, covering many aspects of the phenomenon.

Initially, it focused on the aspect of letting go of grown-up children. We developed the first topic based on consulting sessions with young families who reported feeling "smothered" by their parents. We tried to convey to parents the importance of "reasonable selfishness": parents need to let their adult children go, so that they can create strong, independent families who will, in turn, properly honor and respect their parents.

After giving several seminars with this message and many consultations on this topic, we realized that it was equally important to analyze the other side—the aspect of "leaving" for those adult children who don't want to be let go but instead choose to live off their parents. Often, parents don't immediately recognize the monstrous trap they are being pulled into, as their grown children bring their "significant others" into their home and turn their parents into "scapegoats," blaming parents for their failings.

After lots of sessions and many consultations, we realized that there was one more perspective to consider: what should parents do when their grown-up children got hooked by pseudo specialists and cut ties with their parents (the question which I answered in details in chapter 4 about a Prodigal Son)

My Own Story with My Mother-in-Law

At the very beginning of my married life with my husband, I *had a very difficult relationship with my mother-in-law. I was hurt by her because she had not immediately accepted me as her son's wife; more than that, she did everything she could to prevent our marriage — to be honest, now I understand her very well (I behaved rather disrespectfully towards her). I tried to "set boundaries," demanding my husband choose me over her. I wanted to prove that "a wife comes first." But my husband—bless him—responded simply and firmly:*

"Nadya, this is my mother."

For a long time, my resentment haunted us, and it took a lot of time before I realized something I could have accepted and understood right from the start: she was the first woman who breastfed my husband as a baby and whose warmth he had felt. My distance and hostility toward her primarily affected my relationship with my husband. And if I love my husband, I need to do everything possible to make sure there is no wall between me and his mother.

Marriage is one life for two, and everything in our life belongs to both of us — including our parents. The healing sandwich is a mechanism that works. Start it right at the wedding! It is perfect when the bride publicly thanks the groom's parents for giving her such a man; the groom thanks the bride's parents for their daughter. If there are any resentments, acknowledge them as soon as possible!

I still regret that such a conversation with my second mom didn't happen at the very beginning. Only many years later, I told her: "I am so grateful to you, my dear, for my husband Mikhail, the love of my life! It was very painful for me when you were against me, but I no longer hold any resentment. Please forgive me for all the pain I caused you!" I didn't even finish my sentence because my dear mother-in-law interrupted me: "My dear daughter, forgive me too, honey! If you only knew how peaceful and happy I feel now, when I'm no longer afraid of my old age: I have you, my loving family!"

In Conclusion

Throughout your entire life, until the very last day and your last breath, immerse yourself in gratitude, forgiveness, and blessing. Wishing you wisdom and love!

Legal Disclaimer:

This book is based on my personal opinions, perspectives, and experiences. It is intended for informational and inspirational purposes only. It is not a substitute for professional medical, psychological advice, diagnosis, or treatment. Always seek advice from a qualified healthcare professional if you have any questions regarding medical or mental health conditions. Never disregard professional advice or delay seeking it because of something you have read in this book. The author, editor and publisher assume no responsibility for any actions taken based on the information provided.

Acknowledgments

I am deeply grateful to my husband, Mikhail, who was in my life for 39 years as a devoted husband who loved our family deeply and unconditionally. For 37 of those years, I had the pleasure of being his wife. Thanks to him I evolved and became a wife, a mother, a grandmother, a professional, and simply a woman.

From 1993 to 2021, my husband and I worked together as a team, conducting many seminars, leading training courses, and giving lectures across Russia and abroad. Together we co-authored over 200 articles, books, various manuals, and teaching materials. In 2021, my dear husband passed away, and since that time I have continued our work alone. This book is the first one I have written without him.

I thank my daughter Anastasia, my eldest son-in-law Alexey, who over the years became as dear to me as a son. I am grateful to you for your enormous hearts, your soulful closeness, and boundless love and care. You are our "guardian angels," as my husband always called you.

I thank my daughter Olya, who meticulously and lovingly worked as the chief critic and editor (though unofficially) on the text of this book.

I am grateful to my wonderful grandchildren —the joy and happiness of my heart and my life.

I thank my son Mikhail for his patience and strong support, which I feel deeply after the loss of my husband. In the tragic year of 2021, you, a 19-year-old young man who always saw your father as a rock-solid support, had to mature overnight and take on the full responsibility for taking care of our household, our life, and many new opportunities under difficult circumstances. Your technical help and support in my professional work, as well as in writing this book, have been very valuable.

I am grateful to my former student, Yulia Siminic, now – a very precious friend and editor of the English version of this book. Thank you, dear for your heart and for your deep involvement into the process of making the book flow and read well in English.

I thank my colleagues in the education system in Russia — at the school and university where I worked for nearly three decades. I appreciate your generous heart and warmth.

I am grateful to many people, co-workers, and colleagues with whom we have conducted joint seminars and conferences in various cities and countries on family matters, parent-child relationships, addiction and codependency, and personality development.

I thank my church — in Samara, Alanya, Yerevan, and Miami — wherever I had an opportunity to attend services and be the part of ministry. The feeling of belonging to an amazing community of people always supported me, and it continues supporting me. It means the world to me.

I thank all those people who have turned to me for help, support, and consultation — it is a great joy to see your trust and desire to live in Truth, to witness the changes in your lives, and to be part of your personal and emotional well-being.

I thank my Lord:

- For over 60 years of my life;

- For the happiness of living in the love of a large family, where I began my existence as a daughter and grand-daughter, then sister Nadya, then wife "my Compass," then mother, and now grandmother Nadya;

- For the opportunity to live and engage in the work I love;

- For the chance to know, understand, and carry the Beautiful Truths of Wisdom and Love.

About the Author

Nadezhda (Hope) Telepova is a Doctor of Philosophy (Ph.D.), degree in Psychology.

In 1987, she obtained her Specialist Diploma as a Teacher of English and German as a Second Language from Ussuriysk State Educational University, Russian Federation.

In 2001, she was awarded a Specialist Diploma in Educational Psychology, majoring in Psychology, from the State Autonomous Educational Institution of Higher Education, Moscow City University of Education, Russian Federation.

In 2006, after completing her postgraduate studies, she obtained her Ph.D. in Psychology with the thesis *Psychological Condition and Mechanisms of Development of Personal Self-Esteem of Spouses*. The degree was awarded under the Ministry of Science and Higher Education of the Russian Federation, by resolution of the Dissertation Council at Nizhni Novgorod University of Education.

In 2012, after completing her postgraduate studies, she was awarded the academic degree of Doctor of Psychology with the thesis "Psychological and Educational Conception of Developing Personal Psychological Stability against Factors of Addiction. The degree was conferred under the Ministry of Science and Higher Education of the Russian Federation, by resolution of the Council for the Defense of Theses for Academic Degrees at Nizhni Novgorod State University of Architecture and Civil Engineering.

In 2016, she was awarded the academic title of Associate Professor in Educational Psychology by order of the Ministry of Science and Higher Education of the Russian Federation.

Dr. Hope has a lot of experience as a teacher, professor, lecturer, expert, researcher and counselor at the Universities, Educational Development Centers for teachers, International ACET organization, Rehabilitation centers for addicts.

Dr. Hope contributed to multiple projects dealing with family crisis, addiction and co-addiction, child development, peer pressure, domestic abuse, psychological aspects of HIV+, grief experience, and others. Some of these projects include Samara City Administration Project "Moral Health of the Nation", and Fund "Youth. Family. Morality." Samara Regional Social Organization "Together" for childhood development. Project "Together with family", supported by Fund of President Grants, Social Organization "Salvation" in Samara, "Temerlasi" in Alania, "Fathers'club" in Riga, Vozmozhnost ("opportunity") Asbest center providing help to families and children in crisis.

She conducted multiple seminars in churches of different denominations, educational and social organizations in the cities of the US, Canada, Russia, Kazakhstan, Turkey, Germany, China,

Ukraine, Belarus, Uzbekistan, Lithuania, Latvia, Estonia and others.

She participated in many events all over the world on stress management, parenting, marriage, domestic abuse, addiction and codependency, conflict resolution, ethnic and intercultural dimensions of relationships, communication, crisis prevention (spiritual and psychological issues), death phenomenon, dialogue in teaching process.

Her audience varies from education specialists (schoolteachers, social workers, psychologists), medical workers, church leaders (pastors, youth leaders, group leaders), mission workers, to students and regular people.

She has more than 200 publications, among them 130 Scientific Articles, Educational and Methodical Manuals and Monographs. Most of them are in Russian. She is now busy translating them into English.

Currently Dr.Hope resides in Miami, provides consulting services and different trainings in English and in Russian both online and virtual settings, takes part in different events where she is invited as a speaker and expert; she is working on translation of her works into English and writes new manuals and books. She started learning Spanish as there are a lot of people who speak Spanish where she lives; she believes it is valuable opportunity to connect with people by speaking to them in their native language, especially in her line of work.

You can follow her in Instagram, Facebook, Telegram both in Russian and in English

@telepovs.en

@telepovs

Email dr.Hope.Telepova@gmail.com

Her name **"Nadezhda"** means **"Hope"**

Dr. Hope's several other books are nearly ready for publication: on escaping the blues, on marriage joy, on child development in family and lots of others are in her plans

All of them are based on her experience and practice.

Donations to help Hope in this work may be sent to

PayPal https://www.paypal.me/NadezhdaTelepova

REFERENCES

1. Adler, A. (2002).*Essays on Individual Psychology* (in Russian). Moscow: Cogito-Center.220 p.

2. Berne, E. (1988). *Games People Play. People Who Play Games*(in Russian). Leningrad. 398 p.

3. Berne, E. (1992). *Transactional Analysis and Psychocorrection* (in Russian). St. Petersburg.

4. The Holy Bible. Isaiah 45:9–11; Luke 15:11–32; Deuteronomy 11:26; Psalm 77, 113:9; Hebrews 5:14b; Romans 12:3.

5. Bratus, B. S. (1988). *Anomalies of Personality* (in Russian). Moscow: Mysl. 301 p.

6. Bratus, B. S. *The Meaning of Life. Death* (in Russian). Retrieved from: http://www.funeralportal.ru/library/1535/14799.html

7. Colbert, D. (2009). *Deadly Emotions*. Moscow: Triada Publishing. 304 p.

8. Collins, G. (1988). *Christian Counseling: A Comprehensive Guide*. Dallas: Word Publishing. 712 p.

9. Dye, V. (2006). *The Genesis Process: A Relapse Prevention Workbook for Groups*. Auburn, CA: GAPP.

10. Elkonin, D. B. (1989). *Selected Psychological Works* (in Russian). Moscow: Pedagogy. 560 p.

11. Erikson, E. (1996). *Identity: Youth and Crisis* (in Russian). Moscow.

12. Erikson, E. (2019). *Childhood and Society* (in Russian). St. Petersburg: Piter. 448 p.

13. Feldstein, D. I. (1996). *Features of Leading Activities in Adolescents* (in Russian). Moscow: Institute of Practical Psychology. 304 p.

14. Ferguson, D., Thurman, C. H., & Ferguson, T. (1994). *Intimate Encounters*. Nashville, TN: Janet Thoma Books, Thomas Nelson Inc. 290 p.

15. Frankl, V. (1990). *Man's Search for Meaning* (in Russian). Moscow: Progress. 372 p.

16. Freud, A. (1993). *The Ego and the Mechanisms of Defense* (in Russian). Moscow. 142 p.

17. Fromm, E. (1995). *The Human Condition* (in Russian). Moscow.

18. Gusakov, N. Yu. (2010). *Resentment: Psychogenesis of Destructive Behavior* (in Russian). Yoshkar-Ola: Mari State University. 124 p.

19. Henderson, M. (2002). *Forgiveness: Breaking the Chains of Hatred* (in Russian). Moscow: Biblical-Theological Institute of Apostle Andrew. 264 p.

20. Jaspers, K. (1991). *The Meaning and Purpose of History* (in Russian). Moscow: Politizdat. 527 p.

21. Jung, C. G. *Archetypes and the Collective Unconscious* (in Russian). Moscow: AST Publishers.

22. Kierkegaard, S. (2009). *Philosophical Fragments, or a Fragment of Philosophy* (in Russian). Moscow: St. Thomas Institute.

23. Kohlberg, L., Levine, C., & Hewer, A. (1983). *Moral Stages: A Current Formulation and a Response to Critics*. Basel: Karger. viii, 178 p.

24. Krysko, V. G. (2008). *Ethnic Psychology* (in Russian). Moscow: Academia.

25. Maslow, A. (1970). *Motivation and Personality* (2nd ed.). New York: Harper & Row.

26. Myers, D. (2001). *Social Psychology* (6th ed., revised and expanded) (in Russian). St. Petersburg: Piter. 752 p.

27. Obukhova, L. F. (1996). *Child (Developmental) Psychology: A Textbook* (in Russian). Moscow: Russian Pedagogical Agency. 374 p.

28. Orlov, Yu. M. (1996). *Resentment* (in Russian). Moscow: Imprint-Gulfstream.

29. Osipova, A. A. (2002). *General Psychocorrection: A Textbook* (in Russian). Moscow: Sfera. 510 p.

30. Perls, F. (1993). *Experiments in Self-Awareness Psychology* (in Russian). Moscow.

31. Piaget, J. (1986). *Piaget's Theory / History of Foreign Psychology (1930s–1960s)* (in Russian). Moscow.

32. Piaget, J. (1994). *Speech and Thinking in the Child* (in Russian). Moscow.

33. Rogers, C. (1994). *A Way of Being* (in Russian). Moscow.

34. Ryzhov, V. V. (2011). *Personal Potential / Current Problems in Science and Humanitarian Education* (in Russian). Moscow: Russian-American Institute. 224 p.

35. Shevelenkova, T. D., & Fesenko, T. P. (2005). *Psychological Well-Being of Personality* (in Russian). Psychological Diagnostics, (3), 95–121.

36. Skinner, B. F. (1986). *Operant Behavior* (in Russian). Moscow: History of Foreign Psychology, 1930s–1960s.

37. Smirnov, A. V. (2007). *Leopold Szondi: Fate Analysis* (in Russian). Moscow: Tri Kvadrata.

38. Telepov, M. N., & Telepova, N. N. (2011). *The ABCs of Family (Psychology of Marital Relationships)* (in Russian). Samara: ANPO "ASET". 140 p.

39. Telepov, M. N., & Telepova, N. N. (2013). *Dialogization of the Educational Process as a Factor in Personality Development* (in Russian). Materials of the International Scientific and Practical Conference. Kazan: CHOU VPO "ASO".

40. Telepov, M. N., & Telepova, N. N. (2014). *Personality: Fate or Self-Work* (2nd ed., revised and expanded) (in Russian). Samara: Samara Litfond. 160 p.

41. Telepov, M. N., & Telepova, N. N. (2017). *Questions of Ethnopsychology and Intercultural Interaction* (in Russian). Samara: SFGOU VO MGPU. 96 p.

42. Telepov, M. N., & Telepova, N. N. (2017). *The Algorithm of Love (Psychology of Pre-Marital Relationships)* (3rd ed.) (in Russian). Samara: Telepova N.N. 106 p.

43. Telepova, N. N. (2010). *Forming Psychological Resilience to Addictive Factors* (in Russian). Vestnik Universiteta, (15), 80–84.

44. Telepova, N. N., & Telepov, M. N. (2019). *Dynamics of Resentment Transformation into Destructive Behavior* (in Russian). IV International Penitentiary Forum, Vol. 8, pp. 275–279.

45. Telepova, N., & Telepov, M. (2021). *Correlation Between Psychological Well-Being and the Level of Religious Manifestation at Different Stages of Human Life.* Society. Integration. Education, Vol. 7, pp. 181–188.

46. Telepova, N. N., & Telepov, M. N. (2019). *Aspects of Relationships* (in Russian). Samara: Telepova N.N. 232 p.

47. Vygotsky, L. S. (1984). *The Problem of Age* (Collected Works, Vol. 4) (in Russian). Moscow.

48. Retrieved from: http://www.mobus.com/zdorove/216584.html